FIRST TIME TRAINER FOR THE TOEIC® TEST

Chizuko Tsumatori   Masumi Tahira   Kozue Matsui

(Revised Edition)

Australia • Brazil • Mexico • Singapore • United Kingdom • United States

FIRST TIME TRAINER FOR THE TOEIC® TEST 〈Revised Edition〉
Chizuko Tsumatori, Masumi Tahira, and Kozue Matsui
©2016 Chizuko Tsumatori, Masumi Tahira, and Kozue Matsui

ALL RIGHTS RESERVED. No part of this work covered by the copyright herein may be reproduced, transmitted, stored or used in any form or by any means—graphic, electronic, or mechanical, including but not limited to photocopying, recording, scanning, digitizing, taping, Web distribution, information networks, or information storage and retrieval systems—without the prior written permission of the publisher.

The TOEIC test directions are reprinted by permission of Educational Testing Service, the copyright owner. However, the test questions and any other testing information are provided in their entirety by ASK Publishing Company, Ltd. No endorsement of this publication by Educational Testing Service should be inferred.

For permission to use material from this textbook or product, e-mail to **eltjapan@cengage.com**

Cover photo: アフロ

ISBN: 978-4-86312-293-2

Cengage Learning K.K.
No. 2 Funato Building 5th Floor
1-11-11 Kudankita, Chiyoda-ku
Tokyo 102-0073
Japan

Tel: 03-3511-4392
Fax: 03-3511-4391

はしがき

2016年、TOEICテストに新しい問題が加わりました。そして、正式名称も「TOEIC® Listening & Reading Test」に変わりました。ビジネス英語運用能力を測るテストして、これだけ普及しているTOEICも、時代の変化に対応するため、少しずつ形を変えているのです。そうした柔軟性を持つTOEICの重要性は、これからもしばらく変わらないでしょう。

みなさんも「そろそろ受験しなきゃ」と思っているのではないでしょうか？　と同時に「でも、TOEICって難しいんだよね」とも思っていることでしょう。この感想は、半分あたっていて、半分は間違っています。

TOEIC® Listening & Reading Testは、2時間で200問を解かなければならない、とてもタフな試験です。990点満点中、たとえば900点以上を獲得するとなれば、それは間違いなく「難しい」でしょう。しかし、誰もがいきなりそんな高みを目指すわけではありません。

初級者も上級者も、同じテストを受験するTOEIC® Listening & Reading Testには、初級レベルでも解ける問題が必ず含まれています。その証拠に、難解な文法知識を問う問題は、まず出題されません。文法について言えば、中学・高校で学習した知識で十分に対応できます。、過度に恐れる必要はないのです。

まずは、これまでの学習内容をしっかりブラッシュアップし、自分が解ける問題を確実にものにすることが大切です。そのために、本書では、基礎的な文法知識をおさらいできるようになっています。

ただ、残念ながら、それだけでは足りません。みなさんが「難しい」と感じる要因は、TOEIC特有の「スピード」と「ボリューム」にあります。120分の間、息つく間もなく、大量の英文を聞いて、読んで、解答する——このスピードとボリュームに慣れないと、実力を発揮することは難しいでしょう。

では、慣れるにはどうすればよいのか？　それは、やはり多くの問題を解くしかありません。本書の各ユニットは、全パート（Part 1～7）の問題をまんべんなく解ける構成になっています。さらに、ミニ模試（各50問）のPre-testとPost-test、出題傾向や解法スキルを解説するTipsもあり、TOEIC特有のスタイルに慣れ親しむのに最適な内容になっています。

そして、もうひとつ。「語彙力」を鍛えてほしいと思います。TOEICは、ビジネス要素を多く含むため、みなさんがふだん耳にしない語彙・表現がでてきます。そうした、ビジネスターム、およびTOEIC最頻出の単熟語・フレーズを本書でしっかり身につけてください。巻末の重要語彙リストを使えば、復習も容易です。

TOEIC® Listening & Reading Testは、とてもよくできた試験です。しっかり学習をして、実力が上がれば、その分がきっちりスコアに反映されます。ですから、学習成果を測定する指標として、ふだんの英語学習に取り入れてみてください。TOEIC受験という目標ができることで、モチベーションアップにもつながるはずです。

本書が、「TOEICって難しい」が「案外できるかも」、さらには「英語って楽しい！」に変わるきっかけになってくれれば、それに勝る喜びはありません。

編集部

目次

Pre-test　　　　010
Post-test　　　118
頻出語句リスト　130

		Tips	
Unit 1	**Shopping** 買い物	Part 1 Part 3 and 4	人物写真 情報を関連付けて答える
Unit 2	**Daily Life** 日常生活	Part 1	モノ・風景写真
Unit 3	**Transportation** 交通	Part 2	冒頭の疑問詞がカギ
Unit 4	**Jobs** 職業	Part 2	Yes / No 疑問文への応答は最後まで聞く
Unit 5	**Meals** 食事	Part 2	付加疑問文のコツ
Unit 6	**Communication** コミュニケーション	Part 2	会話が成立するかどうか
Unit 7	**Fun** 楽しみ	Part 2	提案・勧誘・依頼の表現
Unit 8	**Office Work** オフィスワーク	Part 3 and 4	設問先読み
Unit 9	**Meeting** 会議	Part 3 and 4	全体を問う設問
Unit 10	**Travel** 旅行	Part 3 and 4	部分を問う設問
Unit 11	**Finance** お金	Part 3 and 4	未来の行動を問う設問
Unit 12	**Business** ビジネス	Part 3 and 4	言い換え表現

		One Point Grammar	Page
Part 5 and 6	主語を見つける	動詞	**022**
Part 5 and 6 Part 7	セットで覚える 全体を理解しなければならない NOT 問題	名詞	**030**
Part 5 and 6	再帰代名詞に注意	代名詞	**038**
Part 5 and 6 Part 7	形容詞と副詞 2つの文書を参照して解く問題	形容詞と副詞	**046**
Part 5 and 6	時制のヒントとなる語句	時制	**054**
Part 5 and 6 Part 7	主語は人かモノか イントロがヒントになる	受動態・分詞	**062**
Part 5 and 6	動名詞 vs. 不定詞	動名詞と不定詞	**070**
Part 5 and 6 Part 7	助動詞の後には動詞の原形 受取人と差出人をチェック	助動詞	**078**
Part 5 and 6	比較のヒント	比較	**086**
Part 5 and 6	前置詞と接続詞の使い分け	前置詞	**094**
Part 5 and 6	意味のつながりを見極める	接続詞	**102**
Part 5 and 6 Part 7	関係詞を選ぶ手順 文中の単語を言い換える問題	関係詞	**110**

TOEIC® テストとは

TOEIC® テストとは、アメリカの非営利団体 Educational Testing Service が開発したテストで、Test of English for International Communication の略称です。リスニングとリーディングの技能を測定する「TOEIC® テスト」ですが、2016 年 8 月より、正式名称が「TOEIC® Listening and Reading Test」に変更されました。

これは、TOEIC® Speaking and Writing Tests（2007 年開始）とともに、シリーズ全体で 4 技能を測定可能なテストであることを明確に打ち出す戦略だと考えられます。本書が取り扱うのは、TOEIC® Listening and Reading Test のほうです。

さて、その TOEIC® Listening and Reading Test ですが、2015 年度の受験者数が 250 万人を突破。ビジネス界では英語コミュニケーション能力を測るテストとして、事実上のスタンダードです。

同様に人気の高い「英検（実用英語技能検定）」との違いは、「合否を判定するテストではない」という点です。スコアが 10 〜 990 点の間で算出されます（5 点刻み）。また、リスニング 100 問、リーディング 100 問、計 200 問で構成。試験時間はリスニングが約 45 分、リーディングが 75 分の計約 120 分となっており、リスニングとリーディングの間に休憩はありません。2 時間休みなく解答し続けなければならないため、かなりの集中力と体力を要します。

出題される英文は、日常的内容も含みますが、ビジネス要素が非常に強くなっています。この点が、学生のみなさんにとってひとつの壁となるでしょう（本書は、この点を考慮しビジネス語彙や表現も数多く盛り込んでいます）。

▶パート別問題概要

Listening Section				Reading Section		
Part 1	Part 2	Part 3	Part 4	Part 5	Part 6	Part 7
写真描写問題	応答問題	会話問題	説明文問題	短文穴埋め問題	長文穴埋め問題	読解問題
4 択	3 択	4 択	4 択	4 択	4 択	4 択
6 問	25 問	39 問	30 問	30 問	16 問	54 問
約 45 分				75 分		

Part 1　Photographs　写真描写問題

1 枚の写真に対して短い英文が 4 つ読み上げられます。そのなかから写真を最も的確に描写しているものを選ぶ問題。問題用紙には写真しか印刷されていません。解答時間は 1 問あたり約 5 秒です。

Part 2　Question-Response　応答問題

最初の話し手が質問をし、それに対して 2 番目の話し手が 3 つの応答をします。その 3 つのなかから応答として最も適切なものを選びます。質問文と応答文は 1 度しか読まれず、問題冊子にも印刷されていません。Part 1 同様、解答時間は約 5 秒で、5 秒が経過すると次の問題音声が流れます。

Part 3 Conversations 会話問題

2人ないし3人の人物による会話を聞いたあと、その会話に関する3つの設問に答える問題。答えは4つの選択肢から選びます。設問と選択肢は問題冊子に印刷されていますが、会話は印刷されておらず、1度しか読まれません。後半になると、図表を見ながら答える問題も出題されます。解答時間は各設問約8秒ですが、図表問題のみ約12秒に設定されています。

Part 4 Talks 説明文問題

機内アナウンス、ニュース、店内放送、スピーチなど、ひとりの人物による放送を聞き、その内容に関する3つの設問に答える問題。設問と選択肢は問題冊子に印刷されていますが、放送英文は音声のみ。1度しか読まれません。後半に図表を見ながら答える問題も出題されます。解答時間は各設問約8秒。図表問題のみ約12秒に設定されています。

Part 5 Incomplete Sentences 短文穴埋め問題

Part 5からリーディング問題が始まります。ワンセンテンスの英文に設けられた空所に入る適切な語句を4つの選択肢から選ぶ問題。

Part 6 Text Completion 長文穴埋め問題

手紙や記事、Eメールなどの長文に4つの空所が設けられています。それらに入る最も適切な語句・文を、それぞれ4つの選択肢から選ぶ問題。長文の数は4つで、計16問出題されます。

Part 7 Reading Comprehension 読解問題

手紙やEメール、広告、新聞記事、メモなど、さまざまなタイプの長文が提示され、その内容に関する設問に答える問題。4択から最も適切な答えを選びます。ひとつの英文につき、複数の設問が設定されています。また、長文の数によって、以下の3パターンに分類されます。

▶ Single Passage（シングルパッセージ問題）
長文が1つだけ提示され、それについての2〜4問の設問に答える形式。No. 147〜175までの10セット29問が、このシングルパッセージ問題です。

▶ Double Passage（ダブルパッセージ問題）
長文が2つ提示され、それらについて5問の設問に答える形式。No. 176〜185までの2セット10問が、このダブルパッセージ問題です。

▶ Triple Passage（トリプルパッセージ問題）
長文が3つ提示され、それらについて5問の設問に答える形式。No. 186〜200までの3セット15問が、このトリプルパッセージ問題です。

本書の使い方

本書は全12ユニットで構成され、巻頭にPre-test、巻末にPost-testを収録しています。

▶ Pre-testとPost-test

Pre-test、Post-testともに問題数50問、受験時間約33分（リスニング約13分・リーディング20分）のミニ模試となっています（本番のTOEICは200問・120分）。問題形式・内容ともにTOEICテストに倣っており、本番の雰囲気を十分につかめる内容です。
Pre-testは学習前の実力診断、Post-testは最後の学習効果測定にご利用ください。

注意 Pre-testとPost-testの音声は、教師用音源に収録されています。トラック番号が「T」（T-00）となっているので、ご注意ください。

各ユニットの構成

12のユニットにはそれぞれ、TOEIC頻出のテーマが設定されています。そのテーマに沿ったPart 1から7までの模擬問題を25問ずつ解いていくのが、各ユニットの基本構成です。毎回全パートの問題に挑戦することで、TOEICの出題傾向やスピード感への慣れ、そして必要語彙の習得を目指します。

▶ Vocabulary Building

TOEIC公式問題集の徹底分析に加えて、実際の受験経験をもとに頻出語句を15個抽出しました。ここで学習した語句は、同一ユニット内で必ず登場しますし、他ユニットでもくり返し出題されます。そうやって理解の定着を促すとともに、語句単体としてではなく、文脈のなかでの活用法を理解できる仕組みです。

▶ Tips for Part 1〜7

TOEICを受験する上で、必須の知識をパート別に解説。スコアアップに直結する受験スキル、解法テクニックです。ここで学習した内容は、あとに続くTrainingで具体的に演習できるようになっています。

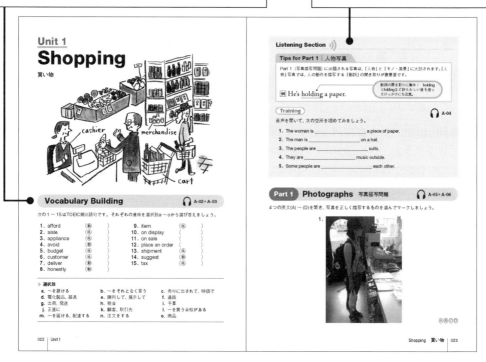

▶ **One Point Grammar**

TOEICに頻出の項目を中心に、間違いやすい文法項目をおさらいします。

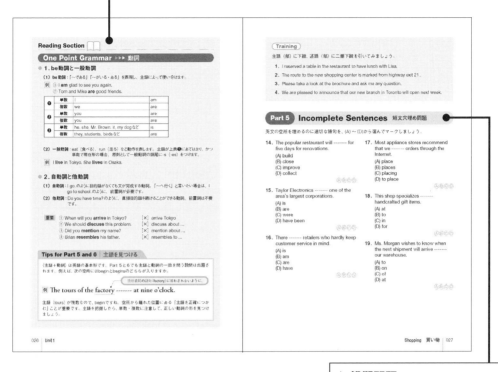

▶ **模擬問題**

Part 1 から 7 までの模擬問題をバランスよく 25 問収録しています。

音声ファイルの無料ダウンロード

https://cengage.jp/elt/Exam/

🎧 A-00 / 🎧 B-00 のアイコンがある本文の音声ファイルをダウンロードできます。

❶ 上記 URL にアクセス、または QR コードをスマートフォンなどのリーダーでスキャン

❷ 本書の表紙画像またはタイトル (FIRST TIME TRAINER FOR THE TOEIC® TEST, Revised Edition) をクリック

❸ 本書のページで 音声ファイル ボタンをクリック

❹ 希望の音声をクリックして音声ファイルをダウンロード

Pre-test

LISTENING TEST T-02 ▶ T-04

In the Listening test, you will be asked to demonstrate how well you understand spoken English. The entire Listening test will last approximately 13 minutes. There are four parts, and directions are given for each part. You must mark your answers on the separate answer sheet. Do not write your answers in your test book.

PART 1

Directions: For each question in this part, you will hear four statements about a picture in your test book. When you hear the statements, you must select the one statement that best describes what you see in the picture. Then find the number of the question on your answer sheet and mark your answer. The statements will not be printed in your test book and will be spoken only one time.

Statement (C), "They're sitting at a table," is the best description of the picture, so you should select answer (C) and mark it on your answer sheet.

1.

Ⓐ Ⓑ Ⓒ Ⓓ

2.

PART 2 🎧 T-05 ▶ T-13

Directions: You will hear a question or statement and three responses spoken in English. They will not be printed in your test book and will be spoken only one time. Select the best response to the question or statement and mark the letter (A), (B), or (C) on your answer sheet.

3. Ⓐ Ⓑ Ⓒ
4. Ⓐ Ⓑ Ⓒ
5. Ⓐ Ⓑ Ⓒ
6. Ⓐ Ⓑ Ⓒ
7. Ⓐ Ⓑ Ⓒ
8. Ⓐ Ⓑ Ⓒ
9. Ⓐ Ⓑ Ⓒ
10. Ⓐ Ⓑ Ⓒ

PART 3 🎧 T-14 ▶ T-20

Directions: You will hear some conversations between two or more people. You will be asked to answer three questions about what the speakers say in each conversation. Select the best response to each question and mark the letter (A), (B), (C), or (D) on your answer sheet. The conversations will not be printed in your test book and will be spoken only one time.

GO ON TO THE NEXT PAGE

11. What are the speakers planning to do?
    (A) Open a store
    (B) Hold a sale
    (C) Have a meal
    (D) Shop for groceries
    Ⓐ Ⓑ Ⓒ Ⓓ

12. Why is the man concerned?
    (A) He is late for lunch.
    (B) He has a limited budget.
    (C) He does not like chicken.
    (D) He missed a museum display.
    Ⓐ Ⓑ Ⓒ Ⓓ

13. What does the woman offer to do?
    (A) Wrap the beef
    (B) Go to the movies
    (C) Cook something special
    (D) Pay for the meal
    Ⓐ Ⓑ Ⓒ Ⓓ

---

14. Who most likely is the man?
    (A) An IT analyst
    (B) A conference host
    (C) A business customer
    (D) A personal assistant
    Ⓐ Ⓑ Ⓒ Ⓓ

15. What is scheduled to happen tomorrow morning?
    (A) A business meeting
    (B) A voicemail upgrade
    (C) A package delivery
    (D) A report deadline
    Ⓐ Ⓑ Ⓒ Ⓓ

16. What does the woman tell the man to do?
    (A) Send a new schedule
    (B) Take down a picture
    (C) Pass on information
    (D) Move a desk
    Ⓐ Ⓑ Ⓒ Ⓓ

Exclusive Today for Members

Purchased Item	Sample Packets Given
Tea:	1
Coffee:	2
Instant Cocoa:	3
Instant Creamer:	4

17. Where most likely does the conversation take place?
    (A) At a store
    (B) At a restaurant
    (C) At a café
    (D) At an outdoor market
    Ⓐ Ⓑ Ⓒ Ⓓ

18. Look at the graphic. How many sample packets will the woman receive?
    (A) 1
    (B) 2
    (C) 3
    (D) 4
    Ⓐ Ⓑ Ⓒ Ⓓ

19. What does the woman say she did last week?
    (A) Signed up for a contest
    (B) Became a store member
    (C) Used automated check-out
    (D) Found a good deal
    Ⓐ Ⓑ Ⓒ Ⓓ

PART 4

T-21 ▶ T-25

Directions: You will hear some talks given by a single speaker. You will be asked to answer three questions about what the speaker says in each talk. Select the best response to each question and mark the letter (A), (B), (C), or (D) on your answer sheet. The talks will not be printed in your test book and will be spoken only one time.

20. Where does the speaker most likely work?
    (A) In a school
    (B) In a fashion shop
    (C) In an office
    (D) In a restaurant

21. What is said about Rebecca Betz?
    (A) She is a recent graduate.
    (B) She has much professional experience.
    (C) She will be helping many coworkers.
    (D) She has purchased new software.

22. What will Thomas do this morning?
    (A) Recruit new food servers
    (B) Guide an individual
    (C) Repair some computers
    (D) Work in the cafeteria

23. What is the main purpose of the telephone message?
    (A) To sell a product
    (B) To collect a payment
    (C) To confirm an appointment
    (D) To get customer feedback

24. What most likely is the speaker's job?
    (A) Property seller
    (B) Employee recruiter
    (C) Furniture store clerk
    (D) Market researcher

25. What does the speaker mean when she says, "Sometimes plans change"?
    (A) The customer could be unavailable.
    (B) The location could be different.
    (C) The service could be ended.
    (D) The goal could be changed.

This is the end of the listening test. Turn to Part 5 in your test book.

GO ON TO THE NEXT PAGE

013

READING TEST

In the Reading test, you will read a variety of texts and answer several different types of reading comprehension questions. The entire Reading test will last 20 minutes. There are three parts, and directions are given for each part. You are encouraged to answer as many questions as possible within the time allowed.

You must mark your answers on the separate answer sheet. Do not write your answers in your test book.

PART 5

Directions: A word or phrase is missing in each of the sentences below. Four answer choices are given below each sentence. Select the best answer to complete the sentence. Then mark the letter (A), (B), (C), or (D) on your answer sheet.

26. The book store ------- at eight o'clock during July and August.
    (A) open
    (B) opens
    (C) opening
    (D) have opened

27. The company needed effective ways to promote ------- new product.
    (A) it
    (B) its
    (C) they
    (D) themselves

28. There was ------- time for us to talk before the meeting.
    (A) short
    (B) quick
    (C) little
    (D) small

29. Alison ------- the cottage near the lake last summer.
    (A) rent
    (B) renting
    (C) to rent
    (D) rented

30. Rose Art Gallery is easily accessible ------- car or train.
    (A) by
    (B) for
    (C) with
    (D) at

31. When traveling, you should give ------- a few days to recover from jet lag.
    (A) you
    (B) your
    (C) yours
    (D) yourself

32. ------- you need more information, please visit our Web site.
(A) Even
(B) Unless
(C) If
(D) Although

33. Please handle this box with -------.
(A) care
(B) cares
(C) careful
(D) carefully

34. Ms. Ropes dealt with the client's complaints very -------.
(A) good
(B) better
(C) bad
(D) well

35. The office has good access to both trains ------- buses.
(A) or
(B) and
(C) nor
(D) with

36. Part-time employees have ------- access to the information.
(A) limit
(B) limits
(C) limited
(D) limitation

GO ON TO THE NEXT PAGE

PART 6

Directions: Read the texts that follow. A word, phrase, or sentence is missing in parts of each text. Four answer choices for each question are given below the text. Select the best answer to complete the text. Then mark the letter (A), (B), (C), or (D) on your answer sheet.

Questions 37-40 refer to the following memo.

To: All employees
From: Martha Jones, Operations Manager
Date: November 16
RE: Company plan

Several departments from our headquarters will be moving into the Tonnis Building next quarter. This ------- should only take about a week.
    37.

The new building is on the west side of the city. ------- .
                                                    38.

We have signed long-term leases for two floors ------- suit our expansion.
                                               39.

More information on this move is coming soon. Department managers ------- of the
                                                                    40.
details promptly.

37. (A) relocation
    (B) account
    (C) delivery
    (D) installation

38. (A) We are pleased that it has been a success.
    (B) It is about 12 kilometers from us.
    (C) Your feedback on the proposal is welcome.
    (D) Only a small $300 deposit is necessary.

39. (A) it
    (B) those
    (C) that
    (D) so

40. (A) had been notified
    (B) have been notified
    (C) are notified
    (D) will be notified

PART 7

Directions: In this part you will read a selection of texts, such as magazine and newspaper articles, e-mails, and instant messages. Each text or set of texts is followed by several questions. Select the best answer for each question and mark the letter (A), (B), (C), or (D) on your answer sheet.

Questions 41-42 refer to the following text message chain.

41. What is suggested about the speakers' printer?

    (A) It is not the latest model.
    (B) It does not work.
    (C) It can use different types of ink cartridges.
    (D) It is a printer for the home.

42. At 11:31 A.M., what does Mr. Greene mean when he writes, "Don't worry about it"?

    (A) The lack of multipacks is not a problem.
    (B) The price of the product is acceptable.
    (C) Mr. Paige needs to calm down.
    (D) Mr. Paige should return to the office.

GO ON TO THE NEXT PAGE

Questions 43-45 refer to the following article.

Cairns Local News

(13 August) A spokesperson for Gaines Events, the entertainment company which organized last weekend's two-day rock festival in Shrove Park, has apologized for canceling the Sunday show.

—[1]—. Heavy rain and strong winds hit the festival site on Saturday evening, and music lovers were wet from head to toe during the first night's performance. —[2]—.

A spokesperson for the company said, "Although we are not responsible for the weather, we do have a responsibility to our customers, to give them the best possible experience. —[3]—. We are sorry for any inconvenience that the cancellation caused them."

"People with tickets for the Sunday show will get their money back", the company promised. —[4]—. Tickets should be mailed to the company's Cairns office.

43. What is the article about?
   (A) Plans for a future festival
   (B) Damage caused by bad weather
   (C) The cancellation of a music event
   (D) A rock-climbing contest

   Ⓐ Ⓑ Ⓒ Ⓓ

44. What has the company promised to do?
   (A) Organize safety training
   (B) Give a refund
   (C) Talk to customers directly
   (D) Clean the venue

   Ⓐ Ⓑ Ⓒ Ⓓ

45. In which of the positions marked [1], [2], [3], and [4] does the following sentence best belong?

   "We regret that so many people were disappointed."

   (A) [1]
   (B) [2]
   (C) [3]
   (D) [4]

   Ⓐ Ⓑ Ⓒ Ⓓ

GO ON TO THE NEXT PAGE

Questions 46-50 refer to the following e-mails.

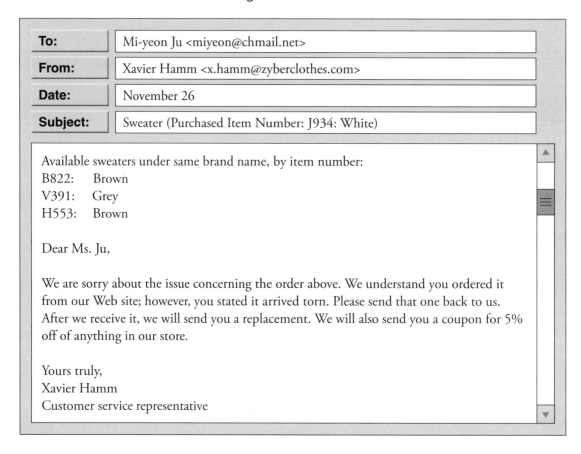

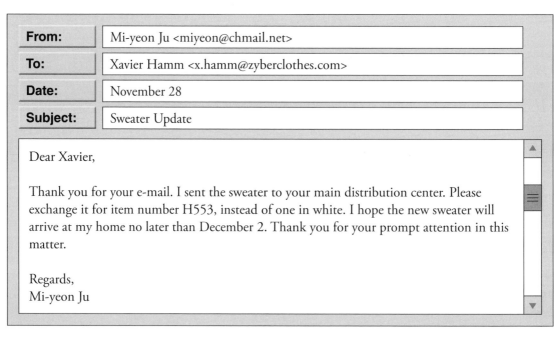

46. Why does Mr. Hamm apologize?
    (A) A clothing piece was unavailable.
    (B) The delivery was late.
    (C) Some goods were wrongly priced.
    (D) A product was damaged.
    Ⓐ Ⓑ Ⓒ Ⓓ

47. What does Mr. Hamm offer to do?
    (A) Update an account
    (B) Provide a discount
    (C) Speak with a manager
    (D) Stamp a coupon
    Ⓐ Ⓑ Ⓒ Ⓓ

48. What color sweater does Ms. Ju hope will arrive by December 2?
    (A) White
    (B) Red
    (C) Grey
    (D) Brown
    Ⓐ Ⓑ Ⓒ Ⓓ

49. Where did Ms. Ju send the original sweater?
    (A) To the store it was purchased at
    (B) To the Web site managers
    (C) To the customer service desk
    (D) To the distribution facility
    Ⓐ Ⓑ Ⓒ Ⓓ

50. In the second e-mail, the word "prompt" in Paragraph 1, Line 3 is closest in meaning to
    (A) factual
    (B) enthusiastic
    (C) quick
    (D) profitable
    Ⓐ Ⓑ Ⓒ Ⓓ

STOP! This is the end of the test. If you finish before time is called, you may go back to Parts 5, 6, and 7 and check your work.

Unit 1
Shopping

買い物

Vocabulary Building 　　　A-02 ▶ A-03

次の1〜15はTOEIC頻出語句です。それぞれの意味を選択肢a〜oから選び答えましょう。

1. afford　　　（動）（　　）
2. aisle　　　（名）（　　）
3. appliance　　（名）（　　）
4. avoid　　　（動）（　　）
5. budget　　　（名）（　　）
6. customer　　（名）（　　）
7. deliver　　　（動）（　　）
8. honestly　　（副）（　　）
9. item　　　（名）（　　）
10. on display　（　　）
11. on sale　　（　　）
12. place an order　（　　）
13. shipment　　（名）（　　）
14. suggest　　（動）（　　）
15. tax　　　（名）（　　）

▶ 選択肢

a. 〜を避ける
b. 〜をそれとなく言う
c. 売りに出されて、特価で
d. 電化製品、器具
e. 陳列して、展示して
f. 通路
g. 出荷、発送
h. 税金
i. 予算
j. 正直に
k. 顧客、取引先
l. 〜を買う余裕がある
m. 〜を届ける、配達する
n. 注文をする
o. 商品

Listening Section

Tips for Part 1 | 人物写真

Part 1（写真描写問題）に出題される写真は、「人物」と「モノ・風景」に大別されます。「人物」写真では、人の動作を描写する「動詞」の聞き取りが最重要です。

例 He's <u>holding</u> a paper.

動詞の聞き取りに集中！ holdingとfoldingなど紛らわしい音を使ったひっかけにも注意。

Training

 A-04

音声を聞いて、次の空所を埋めてみましょう。

1. The woman is _____ a piece of paper.
2. The man is _____ on a hat.
3. The people are _____ suits.
4. They are _____ music outside.
5. Some people are _____ each other.

Part 1　Photographs　写真描写問題　　A-05 ▶ A-06

4つの英文(A)〜(D)を聞き、写真を正しく描写するものを選んでマークしましょう。

1.

Ⓐ Ⓑ Ⓒ Ⓓ

2.

Ⓐ Ⓑ Ⓒ Ⓓ

Part 2 Question-Response 応答問題   A-07 ▶ A-11

問いかけに対する3つの応答(A)〜(C)を聞き、正しいものを選んでマークしましょう。

3. Ⓐ Ⓑ Ⓒ　　4. Ⓐ Ⓑ Ⓒ　　5. Ⓐ Ⓑ Ⓒ　　6. Ⓐ Ⓑ Ⓒ　　7. Ⓐ Ⓑ Ⓒ

Part 3 Short Conversations 会話問題   A-12 ▶ A-13

会話を聞き、3つの設問の答えとして適切なものを(A)〜(D)から選んでマークしましょう。

8. What are the speakers discussing?

   (A) Ordering food
   (B) Purchasing furniture
   (C) Renting an office
   (D) Choosing a rental car

Ⓐ Ⓑ Ⓒ Ⓓ

9. What does the woman have to do herself?

   (A) Count the screws
   (B) Clear the table
   (C) Take the products home
   (D) Put things together

Ⓐ Ⓑ Ⓒ Ⓓ

10. What will the woman probably do next?

    (A) Pay for the items
    (B) Leave the counter
    (C) Buy some tools
    (D) Read the instructions

Ⓐ Ⓑ Ⓒ Ⓓ

Tips for Part 3 and 4 | 情報を関連付けて答える

Part 3と4では、問題冊子に図表が印刷された「図表問題」が出題されます。このタイプの問題では、音声（会話・トーク）と図表の内容を関連付けて解答します。音声だけ、あるいは図表だけでは正答できないように作られています。

図表例

Today's Presentation	
Time	**Presenter**
9:00 A.M.–10:00 A.M.	Ms. Smith
10:30 A.M.–11:30 A.M.	Mr. Asensio
1:30 P.M.–2:30 P.M.	Ms. Jaspers
2:45 P.M.–3:45 P.M.	Mr. Vázquez

設問例

Look at the graphic. Who will be the first presenter?

(A) Ms. Smith
(B) Mr. Asensio
(C) Ms. Jaspers
(D) Mr. Vázquez

Ms. Smithが正解のように思えるが、会話・トークのなかで、予定変更が伝えられるなど、図表だけでは正答できないようになっている。

Part 4　Short Talks　説明文問題　　A-14 ▶ A-15

説明文を聞き、3つの設問の答えとして適切なものを(A)〜(D)から選んでマークしましょう。

11. Where most likely is the announcement being made?
    (A) In a cafeteria
    (B) At a food warehouse
    (C) At a city festival
    (D) In a store

12. Look at the graphic. What is indicated about the apples?
    (A) They are organic.
    (B) They are discounted.
    (C) They are new.
    (D) They are popular.

13. What are listeners advised to do?
    (A) Talk to a store employee
    (B) Pick out a sample
    (C) Shop online from home
    (D) Select a membership card

Shopping　買い物

Reading Section

One Point Grammar ▶▶▶ 動詞

● **1. be動詞と一般動詞**

〔1〕 be動詞：「～である」「～がいる・ある」を表現し、主語によって使い分けます。

例 ① I **am** glad to see you again.
② Tom and Mike **are** good friends.

❶	単数	I	am
	複数	we	are
❷	単数	you	are
	複数	you	are
❸	単数	he, she, Mr. Brown, it, my dog など	is
	複数	they, students, birds など	are

〔2〕 一般動詞：eat（食べる）、run（走る）など動作を表します。主語が上表❸にあてはまり、かつ単数で現在形の場合、原則として一般動詞の語尾に -s（-es）をつけます。

例 I **live** in Tokyo. She **lives** in Osaka.

● **2. 自動詞と他動詞**

〔1〕 自動詞：I go. のように目的語がなくても文が完成する動詞。「～へ行く」と言いたい場合は、I go to school. のように、前置詞が必要です。

〔2〕 他動詞：Do you have time? のように、直接目的語を続けることができる動詞。前置詞は不要です。

重要
① When will you **arrive** in Tokyo?　　［✕］ arrive Tokyo
② We should **discuss** this problem.　　［✕］ discuss about ...
③ Did you **mention** my name?　　［✕］ mention about ...
④ Brian **resembles** his father.　　［✕］ resembles to ...

Tips for Part 5 and 6 | 主語を見つける

〈主語＋動詞〉は英語の基本形です。Part 5と6でも主語と動詞の一致を問う設問は出題されます。例えば、次の空所にはbeginとbeginsのどちらが入りますか。

> 空所直前の語句（factory）に惑わされないように。

例 The tours of the factory ------- at nine o'clock.

主語（tours）が複数なので、beginですね。空所から離れた位置にある「主語を正確につかむ」ことが重要です。主語を把握したら、単数・複数に注意して、正しい動詞の形を見つけましょう。

Training

主語（部）に下線、述語（部）に二重下線を引いてみましょう。

1. I reserved a table in the restaurant to have lunch with Lisa.
2. The route to the new shopping center is marked from highway exit 21.
3. Please take a look at the brochure and ask me any question.
4. We are pleased to announce that our new branch in Toronto will open next week.

Part 5 Incomplete Sentences 短文穴埋め問題

英文の空所を埋めるのに適切な語句を、(A)〜(D)から選んでマークしましょう。

14. The popular restaurant will ------- for five days for renovations.
(A) build
(B) close
(C) improve
(D) collect

15. Taylor Electronics ------- one of the area's largest corporations.
(A) is
(B) are
(C) were
(D) have been

16. There ------- retailers who hardly keep customer service in mind.
(A) is
(B) am
(C) are
(D) have

17. Most appliance stores recommend that we ------- orders through the Internet.
(A) place
(B) places
(C) placing
(D) to place

18. This shop specializes ------- handcrafted gift items.
(A) at
(B) to
(C) in
(D) for

19. Ms. Morgan wishes to know when the next shipment will arrive ------- our warehouse.
(A) to
(B) on
(C) of
(D) at

Shopping 買い物

Part 6 Text Completion 長文穴埋め問題

英文の4つの空所を埋めるのに適切な語句を、(A)～(D)から選んでマークしましょう。

Questions 20-23 refer to the following e-mail.

To: Ji-eun Choi
From: Excern Electronics
Date: July 8
Subject: Sale

Dear Ms. Choi,

We are writing to inform you of a great new ------- . Right now, many of the items in
　　　　　　　　　　　　　　　　　　　　　　　　20.
our store are up to 15 % off their ------- prices. This means our already-low prices are
　　　　　　　　　　　　　　　　　 21.
even better than ever! ------- .
　　　　　　　　　　 22.

This sale only lasts through July 31. This is something that you will not want to

------- . Visit either our stores or our Web site.
23.

Yours truly,

Promotions
Excern Electronics

---

20. (A) location
　　　(B) investment
　　　(C) opportunity
　　　(D) performance

21. (A) normal
　　　(B) normally
　　　(C) normalize
　　　(D) normalization

22. (A) You do not have to be a store member to benefit.
　　　(B) Please pay promptly to avoid any late fees.
　　　(C) Each coupon must be used before its expiration date.
　　　(D) Some of the best items are in our vegetables aisle.

23. (A) raise
　　　(B) control
　　　(C) miss
　　　(D) block

Part 7 · Reading Comprehension 読解問題

文書を読み、2つの設問の答えとして適切なものを(A)〜(D)から選んでマークしましょう。

Questions 24-25 refer to the following text message chain.

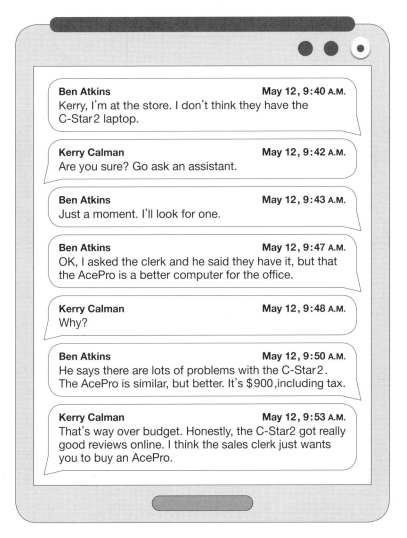

24. At 9:43 A.M., what does Mr. Atkins mean when he writes, "I'll look for one"?

    (A) He will check for a price tag.
    (B) He will try to find a store clerk.
    (C) He will search for a different computer.
    (D) He will research other stores in the area.

    Ⓐ Ⓑ Ⓒ Ⓓ

25. What is suggested about Ms. Calman?

    (A) She agrees with the sales clerk.
    (B) She works for Mr. Atkins.
    (C) She does not read online reviews.
    (D) She cannot afford an AcePro.

    Ⓐ Ⓑ Ⓒ Ⓓ

Unit 2
Daily Life

日常生活

Vocabulary Building

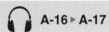

次の1～15はTOEIC頻出語句です。それぞれの意味を選択肢a～oから選び答えましょう。

1. annual　　　　（形）（　　）
2. appointment　（名）（　　）
3. battery　　　（名）（　　）
4. brochure　　（名）（　　）
5. confirm　　　（動）（　　）
6. degree　　　（名）（　　）
7. electricity　（名）（　　）
8. I'm afraid ～　　（　　）
9. insurance　　（名）（　　）
10. provide　　（動）（　　）
11. receptionist（名）（　　）
12. registration（名）（　　）
13. temperature（名）（　　）
14. traffic　　（名）（　　）
15. vehicle　　（名）（　　）

▶ 選択肢

a. 交通（量）
b. 年1回の、毎年の
c. パンフレット
d. 登録
e. 受付係
f. （好ましくないことについて）～と思う
g. 保険
h. 車両、乗り物
i. （病院などの）予約、（会う）約束
j. ～を確認する
k. 温度、気温
l. ～を提供する
m. 電池
n. 電気
o. 度（温度の単位）

Listening Section

Tips for Part 1 | モノ・風景写真

「モノ・風景写真」では、位置関係がよく問われます。next to（〜の横に）、in front of（〜の前に）、side by side（並んで）といった表現に注意して、「何がどこにあるのか」を聞き取ることが重要です。

> 位置関係をイメージしながら聞く。

例 The cars are parked in front of the buildings.

Training

絵を見て、空欄にあてはまる語句を下から選び、音声で確認しましょう（2回使うものもあり）。

1. There are two phones _____ the desk.
2. There is a plant _____ the desk.
3. There is a trash can _____ the desk.
4. A picture is hanging _____ the wall.

選択肢 under / next to / on

Part 1 Photographs 写真描写問題

4つの英文(A) 〜 (D)を聞き、写真を正しく描写するものを選んでマークしましょう。

1.

Ⓐ Ⓑ Ⓒ Ⓓ

2.

ⒶⒷⒸⒹ

Part 2 Question-Response 応答問題   A-21 ▶ A-25

問いかけに対する3つの応答(A) ～ (C)を聞き、正しいものを選んでマークしましょう。

3. ⒶⒷⒸ   4. ⒶⒷⒸ   5. ⒶⒷⒸ   6. ⒶⒷⒸ   7. ⒶⒷⒸ

Part 3 Short Conversations 会話問題   A-26 ▶ A-27

会話を聞き、3つの設問の答えとして適切なものを(A) ～ (D)から選んでマークしましょう。

8. Why is the man calling?
   (A) To market a new service
   (B) To confirm a schedule
   (C) To provide an address
   (D) To request a payment

   ⒶⒷⒸⒹ

9. What does the woman ask the man about?
   (A) The date of a conference
   (B) The phone number of a clinic
   (C) The length of an appointment
   (D) The person she will meet

   ⒶⒷⒸⒹ

10. What did Simmons Clinic send last week?
    (A) The clinic's information
    (B) Insurance plans
    (C) A medical bill
    (D) New medicine

    ⒶⒷⒸⒹ

Part 4 Short Talks 説明文問題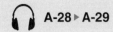

説明文を聞き、3つの設問の答えとして適切なものを(A)～(D)から選んでマークしましょう。

11. What is predicted for the rest of the day?

(A) Sunshine
(B) Rain
(C) Strong heat
(D) Snow

Ⓐ Ⓑ Ⓒ Ⓓ

12. When will a change take place today?

(A) At 9:00 A.M.
(B) At 10:00 A.M.
(C) At 12:00 noon
(D) At 1:00 P.M.

Ⓐ Ⓑ Ⓒ Ⓓ

13. What will listeners hear next?

(A) A celebrity interview
(B) A daily business report
(C) Traffic conditions
(D) A piece of music

Ⓐ Ⓑ Ⓒ Ⓓ

Reading Section

One Point Grammar ▶▶▶ 名詞

● 1. 可算名詞と不可算名詞

〔1〕 **可算名詞**：tableやbatteryのように「数えられる名詞」。ひとつの場合はa(an)やtheをつけ、ふたつ以上の場合は語尾に-s（-es）をつけて複数形で使います。

例 ① There is **a table** near the window.
② We are running short of **batteries**.

〔2〕 **不可算名詞**：furnitureやequipmentのように「数えられない名詞」。a(an)をつけたり、複数形にしたりしません。

例 Some **furniture** was moved.

● 2. manyとmuch／fewとlittle

〔1〕 **many**や**(a) few**：可算名詞といっしょに使います。

例 ① I'm looking forward to talking with **many** of you.
② Over the next **few** weeks, we'll be hosting various events.

〔2〕 **much**や**(a) little**：不可算名詞といっしょに使います。

例 ① I don't have **much** time to talk now.
② He has had **a little** experience in this field.

> **重要** 名詞の主な語尾
> -ment   -tion, -sion   -ee, -er
> -ist   -ent   -ity
> -ship   -ism, -ness

Tips for Part 5 and 6 ｜ セットで覚える

名詞に関しては日頃から語彙を増やすことに加え、熟語のようにセットで使われる表現を覚えておくことがPart 5と6の攻略に役立ちます。例えば、beyond repairのrepair部分が空所になるような問題が出題されます。

> beyond repairとセットで覚えておけば、すぐに解答できる。

例 The damage was beyond -------.

Training

[　] 内の名詞を挿入するのに適切な個所に矢印をつけましょう。

1. We need to purchase office.　　　　　　　　　　　[equipment]
2. They made an official about his resignation.　　　[announcement]
3. They released a new of products yesterday.　　　[line]
4. Ask our for more information.　　　　　　　　　　[receptionist]

Part 5　Incomplete Sentences　短文穴埋め問題

英文の空所を埋めるのに適切な語句を、(A) 〜 (D) から選んでマークしましょう。

14. The ad campaign had the desired ------- of bringing in new customers.

(A) affect
(B) effective
(C) effectively
(D) effect

Ⓐ Ⓑ Ⓒ Ⓓ

15. ------- the survey, half of the respondents remain single.

(A) As far as
(B) According to
(C) In addition
(D) No matter how

Ⓐ Ⓑ Ⓒ Ⓓ

16. Bridge Hotel has been enjoying a ------- for customer service.

(A) reputation
(B) estimation
(C) completion
(D) compensation

Ⓐ Ⓑ Ⓒ Ⓓ

17. The old heater was replaced during routine ------- last week.

(A) maintenance
(B) influence
(C) residence
(D) emergence

Ⓐ Ⓑ Ⓒ Ⓓ

18. The mall is easily accessible to all the ------- of East and North Town.

(A) popular
(B) popularity
(C) population
(D) popularly

Ⓐ Ⓑ Ⓒ Ⓓ

Daily Life　日常生活　035

Part 6 Text Completion 長文穴埋め問題

英文の4つの空所を埋めるのに適切な語句を、(A)～(D)から選んでマークしましょう。

Questions 19-22 refer to the following article.

Greenville (April 24)—This Saturday at 8:00 A.M., the downtown area will be filled with sports fans. That is because it ------- the ninth annual International Bicycle Race.
　　　　　　　　　　　　　　　　　　　　　　19.

This is one of the most exciting ------- in the area. The cyclist will race through
　　　　　　　　　　　　　　　　　20.
downtown, ------- will be closed to vehicles. Admission is free, but it is probably a
　　　　　　21.
good idea to come before 6:00 A.M. ------- .
　　　　　　　　　　　　　　　　　22.

---

19. (A) had hosted
    (B) will host
    (C) would have hosted
    (D) had been hosting

20. (A) athletes
    (B) fields
    (C) competitions
    (D) sponsors

21. (A) they
    (B) it
    (C) which
    (D) that

22. (A) We will respond to your feedback as soon as we can.
    (B) Participation in the event requires advance registration.
    (C) The others have to pay a higher entrance fee.
    (D) The best viewing spots are usually taken quickly.

Tips for Part 7 | 全体を理解しなければならないNOT問題

Part 7（読解問題）には〈NOT問題〉というものが出題されます。たとえば、What is NOT stated in the document?という設問で、パッセージの中で述べられていないことを選ばなければいけません。

> このようにNOT部分が大文字になっている。

例 **What is NOT stated in the document?**

述べられていないことは、パッセージ全体の内容を把握しないと答えられません。そのため解答に時間もかかり、難しい問題です。

Part 7 Reading Comprehension 読解問題

文書を読み、3つの設問の答えとして適切なものを(A) ～ (D)から選んでマークしましょう。

Questions 23-25 refer to the following notice.

Are you the person we are looking for?

Every day, dogs and cats are left on the streets of Chester. —[1]—. Here at Happy Paws Animal Center, we take care of any pets that need help. However, what we want most is to find new families for these animals.

—[2]—. Rescued pets are often nervous around people, so potential owners should be kind and calm. You need to have a clean and safe house with outside space, and in the case of dogs, enough free time to walk them twice a day.

—[3]—. Apply by sending us a message, using the form below, if you think your family could offer a pet a new home. —[4]—. Simply click the photos below to find out more. Thank you!

23. What is the purpose of this notice?
    (A) To advertise a new pet store
    (B) To advise dog training
    (C) To find new homes for animals
    (D) To promote a photo contest

24. What is NOT a stated requirement for participants?
    (A) Enough space to sleep
    (B) A patient personality
    (C) A home with a yard
    (D) Plenty of spare time

25. In which of the positions marked [1], [2], [3], and [4] does the following sentence best belong?

    "Get to know our charming animals better."

    (A) [1]
    (B) [2]
    (C) [3]
    (D) [4]

Unit 3
Transportation

交通

Vocabulary Building

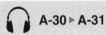 A-30 ▶ A-31

次の1〜15はTOEIC頻出語句です。それぞれの意味を選択肢a〜oから選び答えましょう。

1. aircraft (名) (　　)
2. board (動) (　　)
3. commuter (名) (　　)
4. concern (名) (　　)
5. consider X Y (動) (　　)
6. delay (名/動) (　　)
7. depart (動) (　　)
8. due to 〜 (　　)
9. get (動) (　　)
10. hand X to Y (動) (　　)
11. on time (　　)
12. park (動) (　　)
13. passenger (名) (　　)
14. public transportation (名) (　　)
15. subway (名) (　　)

▶ 選択肢
- a. 公共交通機関
- b. 着く、到着する
- c. 時間通りに
- d. 出発する
- e. 乗客
- f. 航空機
- g. 通勤［通学］者
- h. 〜が原因で
- i. 地下鉄
- j. 〜を駐車する
- k. 心配（事）
- l. （飛行機・バスなど）に乗り込む
- m. 遅延／〜を延期する
- n. XをYと考える
- o. XをYに手渡す

Listening Section

Tips for Part 2 | 冒頭の疑問詞がカギ

Part 2（応答問題）の問題のうち10問前後が、疑問詞で始まります。正答するには冒頭を聞き逃さないことが必須です。

　　　　　　　最初の疑問詞を必ず聞き取る！

例 **Where** is the post office?

疑問詞に応じて、場所、日時、人（職業）など、何を答えるべきなのかを予想しながら、応答選択肢を聞きましょう。

Training A-32

空欄に入る疑問詞を選択肢から選びましょう。答えは音声で確認してください。

1. Q _____ is the post office? → Ⓐ At the next corner.
2. Q _____ does the coffee shop open? → Ⓐ 9 A.M.
3. Q _____ are you staying there? → Ⓐ For two weeks.
4. Q _____ is Mr. Green? → Ⓐ He is our supervisor.
5. Q _____ did you talk about? → Ⓐ Nothing special.

| 選択肢 | How long / What / When / Where / Who

Part 1　**Photographs**　写真描写問題　 A-33 ▶ A-34

4つの英文(A)〜(D)を聞き、写真を正しく描写するものを選んでマークしましょう。

1.

Ⓐ Ⓑ Ⓒ Ⓓ

2.

Ⓐ Ⓑ Ⓒ Ⓓ

Part 2 Question-Response 応答問題   A-35 ▶ A-39

問いかけに対する3つの応答(A) 〜 (C)を聞き、正しいものを選んでマークしましょう。

3. Ⓐ Ⓑ Ⓒ   4. Ⓐ Ⓑ Ⓒ   5. Ⓐ Ⓑ Ⓒ   6. Ⓐ Ⓑ Ⓒ   7. Ⓐ Ⓑ Ⓒ

Part 3 Short Conversations 会話問題   A-40 ▶ A-41

会話を聞き、3つの設問の答えとして適切なものを(A) 〜 (D)から選んでマークしましょう。

CITY STATION
Terminal 1: Subway
Terminal 2: Buses
Terminal 3: Taxis
Terminal 4: Ferries

8. Who are the speakers going to see?
   (A) A customer
   (B) A manager
   (C) A supplier
   (D) A coworker

   Ⓐ Ⓑ Ⓒ Ⓓ

9. Look at the graphic. What terminal will the speakers use?
   (A) Terminal 1
   (B) Terminal 2
   (C) Terminal 3
   (D) Terminal 4

   Ⓐ Ⓑ Ⓒ Ⓓ

10. What is the woman concerned about?
    (A) Damaging bags
    (B) Packing gifts
    (C) Convincing a supervisor
    (D) Bringing items

    Ⓐ Ⓑ Ⓒ Ⓓ

Part 4　Short Talks　説明文問題　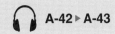

説明文を聞き、3つの設問の答えとして適切なものを(A)～(D)から選んでマークしましょう。

11. Where is the announcement being made?

(A) At a ferry terminal
(B) At a train station
(C) At a bus center
(D) At an airport

　Ⓐ Ⓑ Ⓒ Ⓓ

12. What is the new departure gate?

(A) Gate 4
(B) Gate 5
(C) Gate 6
(D) Gate 7

　Ⓐ Ⓑ Ⓒ Ⓓ

13. What does the speaker mean when he says, "There's no cause for concern"?

(A) A refund will be given.
(B) A mistake will be avoided.
(C) A time will not change.
(D) An assistant is available.

　Ⓐ Ⓑ Ⓒ Ⓓ

Reading Section

One Point Grammar ▶▶▶ 代名詞

● 1. 代名詞の形

代名詞は、通常直前にある名詞の代わりをします。主語か目的語か、単数か複数かなどによって形を変えます。

例
① This is Ken. **He** is my friend.　　　　［主語］
② I've known **him** for long.　　　　　　［目的語］
③ He lost **his** key yesterday.　　　　　　［所有を表す］
④ This baggage is **mine**, not **yours**.　　［「～のもの」という意味］

		主語	目的語	所有格	所有代名詞	再帰代名詞
単数		I	me	my	mine	myself
複数		we	us	our	ours	ourselves
単数		you	you	your	yours	yourself
複数						yourselves
単数		he / she / it	him / her / it	his / her / its	his / hers / —	himself / herself / itself
複数		they	them	their	theirs	themselves

※このほか、itやthat、this、theyなどが、何を指しているのか正確につかみましょう。

● 2. otherとanother

otherは「ほかの」もの、anotherは「もうひとつ」であることに注意。

例
① I have two bags. One is red and **the other** is white.
② Can I get **another**?

※ othersは、ほかのものが複数ある場合や、「他人」「人々」という意味。

重要　We've known **each other** for more than 20 years.
※ one anotherも同意。

Tips for Part 5 and 6 ｜ 再帰代名詞に注意

Part 5と6では毎回、代名詞の問題が出題されます。しっかり覚えて得点源にしましょう。その代名詞が何を指しているのかに注意して解答を選ぶこと、また再帰代名詞（myself／yourself／themselves など）の使い方を理解しておくことがポイントです。

（meとmyselfの違いに注意。）

例　I'd like to introduce <u>myself</u>.
　　Mr. Brown introduced himself to <u>me</u>.

> **Training**

( )内の2語のうち、適切なほうを丸で囲みましょう。

1. Alison is old enough to look after (her / herself).
2. Brian is retiring, ending (his / himself) twenty-year career.
3. Help (you / yourself) to anything on the table.
4. Traveling on (your / yourselves) own can be lonely.

Part 5　Incomplete Sentences 短文穴埋め問題

英文の空所を埋めるのに適切な語句を、(A)〜(D)から選んでマークしましょう。

14. For further information, please visit ------- Web site.
    (A) us
    (B) we
    (C) our
    (D) ourselves

15. Oliver went to the station earlier, and ------- is still waiting in line for tickets.
    (A) he
    (B) his
    (C) him
    (D) himself

16. Commuters should leave ------- cars at home and use public transportation.
    (A) they
    (B) their
    (C) theirs
    (D) them

17. The company is asking ------- employees to park their cars in the designated area.
    (A) they
    (B) them
    (C) it
    (D) its

18. Mr. Sato and Ms. Lee have known ------- since they were university students.
    (A) other one
    (B) each other
    (C) another one
    (D) any other

19. Although Amy is always on time, she does not consider ------- a punctual person.
    (A) she
    (B) her
    (C) hers
    (D) herself

Part 6 Text Completion 長文穴埋め問題

英文の4つの空所を埋めるのに適切な語句を、(A) ～ (D)から選んでマークしましょう。

Questions 20-23 refer to the following notice.

Province Transportation Department

Attention Drivers

Highway 9 will be closed on March 25, between Exit 13 and Exit 27. This is an unavoidable closure. Know that ------- (20.) will continue until the last week in November. The traffic suspension applies to all lanes while the roadwork is being carried out.

Drivers ------- (21.) by this project must find different routes. Online maps and similar services may be helpful for this. ------- (22.) .

We thank you for your ------- (23.) during this time.

---

20. (A) it
(B) you
(C) theirs
(D) mine

21. (A) will affect
(B) affecting
(C) affected
(D) have been affected

22. (A) We recognize your efforts in reducing accidents.
(B) You must follow these workplace safety rules.
(C) You are advised to give yourselves extra time.
(D) The month of January was certainly a very busy one.

23. (A) value
(B) patience
(C) shipment
(D) management

Part 7 Reading Comprehension 読解問題

文書を読み、2つの設問の答えとして適切なものを(A)〜(D)から選んでマークしましょう。

Questions 24-25 refer to the following text message chain.

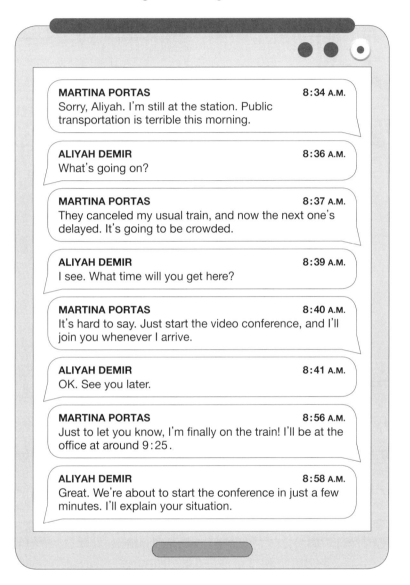

24. At 8:40 A.M., what does Ms. Portas mean when she writes, "It's hard to say"?

(A) Some information is private.
(B) A word is difficult to pronounce.
(C) She does not understand a question.
(D) She does not know an answer.

Ⓐ Ⓑ Ⓒ Ⓓ

25. What time is the video conference most likely to start?

(A) At 8:35 A.M.
(B) At 8:40 A.M.
(C) At 9:00 A.M.
(D) At 9:25 A.M.

Ⓐ Ⓑ Ⓒ Ⓓ

Transportation 交通 | 045

Unit 4
Jobs

職業

Vocabulary Building

A-44 ▶ A-45

次の1～15はTOEIC頻出語句です。それぞれの意味を選択肢a～oから選び答えましょう。

1. candidate (名) (　　)
2. coworker (名) (　　)
3. department (名) (　　)
4. duty (名) (　　)
5. head (名) (　　)
6. human resources (　　)
7. interview (名) (　　)
8. mention (動) (　　)
9. opening (名) (　　)
10. position (名) (　　)
11. purpose (名) (　　)
12. résumé (名) (　　)
13. sales representative (　　)
14. submit (動) (　　)
15. transfer (動) (　　)

▶ 選択肢
- a. 同僚
- b. 職、仕事
- c. （組織の）長、リーダー
- d. 職務、義務
- e. ～に言及する
- f. 営業担当、販売代理人
- g. 志望者、候補者
- h. 人事部（課）、人材
- i. 部署、課
- j. 履歴書
- k. 目的
- l. ～を提出する
- m. 面接
- n. 転任する、転勤する
- o. 欠員、就職口

Listening Section

Tips for Part 2 | Yes / No疑問文への応答は最後まで聞く

Do / Does ... ? や Will / Can ... ? で始まる Yes / No疑問文には、yesやnoの応答が基本ですが、そのあともしっかり聞いてから解答してください。主語や時制をあえてずらした、ひっかけがよく見られます。

例 Will Mr. Hall attend the conference?
  [×] No, he didn't. — 時制が違う！
  [×] Yes, I will.
  [○] Yes, he will. — 主語が違う！

Training A-46

空所にYesとNoのどちらが入るか考えましょう。答えは音声で確認してください。

1. Q Can I use this computer? → A _____, it's broken.
2. Q Are you going to the third floor? → A _____, but later.
3. Q Have you worked in China? → A _____, briefly.
4. Q Have you ever been to Singapore? → A _____, but I'd love to.

Part 1　Photographs 写真描写問題　A-47 ▶ A-48

4つの英文(A)～(D)を聞き、写真を正しく描写するものを選んでマークしましょう。

1.

Ⓐ Ⓑ Ⓒ Ⓓ

Jobs　職業 | 047

2.

Ⓐ Ⓑ Ⓒ Ⓓ

Part 2　Question-Response　応答問題　 A-49 ▶ A-52

問いかけに対する3つの応答(A)～(C)を聞き、正しいものを選んでマークしましょう。

3. Ⓐ Ⓑ Ⓒ　　4. Ⓐ Ⓑ Ⓒ　　5. Ⓐ Ⓑ Ⓒ　　6. Ⓐ Ⓑ Ⓒ

Part 3　Short Conversations　会話問題　 A-53 ▶ A-54

会話を聞き、3つの設問の答えとして適切なものを(A)～(D)から選んでマークしましょう。

7. What are the speakers mainly discussing?

   (A) Career development
   (B) Business performance
   (C) A new coworker
   (D) Education qualifications

   Ⓐ Ⓑ Ⓒ Ⓓ

8. What does the man plan to do this winter?

   (A) Update his résumé
   (B) Advise engineers
   (C) Change his type of work
   (D) Give a business talk

   Ⓐ Ⓑ Ⓒ Ⓓ

9. What does the woman say about Frances Parker?

   (A) She opened several new branches.
   (B) She leads her own company.
   (C) She may provide some assistance.
   (D) She transferred into a different field.

   Ⓐ Ⓑ Ⓒ Ⓓ

Part 4 Short Talks 説明文問題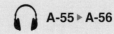

説明文を聞き、3つの設問の答えとして適切なものを(A)～(D)から選んでマークしましょう。

10. What is the main purpose of the message?
- (A) To market a product
- (B) To open an account
- (C) To change an arrangement
- (D) To get a reference

Ⓐ Ⓑ Ⓒ Ⓓ

11. When does SPG Plumbing Corporation normally open for business?
- (A) At 7:00 A.M.
- (B) At 8:00 A.M.
- (C) At 8:30 A.M.
- (D) At 9:30 A.M.

Ⓐ Ⓑ Ⓒ Ⓓ

12. What is Mr. Ming asked to do?
- (A) Contact the caller
- (B) Wait for an e-mail
- (C) Post a schedule
- (D) Confirm an address

Ⓐ Ⓑ Ⓒ Ⓓ

Reading Section

One Point Grammar ▶▶▶ 形容詞と副詞

● **1. 形容詞**

人やモノの性質・状態を表し、名詞を修飾します。

例 ① This restaurant is **popular** in the town.
② He is a **popular** singer in the town.

● **2. 副詞**

主に動詞を修飾しますが、形容詞、副詞、文全体も修飾します。

例 ① She speaks **quietly**.
② They are twins, but they look **quite** different.
③ The project went **quite** well.
④ **Unfortunately**, the project failed.

Tips for Part 5 and 6 | 形容詞と副詞

形容詞と副詞のどちらが適切かを選ばせる問題も頻出です。その場合、空所前後の品詞をチェックし、「名詞であれば形容詞」、「動詞・形容詞・副詞であれば副詞」の判断をします。次の空所にはextremeとextremelyのどちらが適切でしょうか。

> 名詞(risks)が直後にあるので、形容詞が入ると判断する。

例 The team preferred to take ------- risks.

Training

(　)内の2語のうち、適切なほうを丸で囲みましょう。

1. Don't touch it. That's an extremely (dangerous / dangerously) chemical.
2. Mr. Yang is (particular / particularly) interested in the position of chief editor.
3. Everyone at the convention should wear (formal / formally) clothes.
4. He has (successful / successfully) managed his department until now.

Part 5 Incomplete Sentences 短文穴埋め問題

英文の空所を埋めるのに適切な語句を、(A)～(D)から選んでマークしましょう。

13. Mr. Garcia was one of the most ------- candidates for the position.
    (A) occupied
    (B) qualified
    (C) stated
    (D) figured

14. The librarian asked visitors to speak ------- when in the reading room.
    (A) quiet
    (B) quieter
    (C) quietness
    (D) quietly

15. The reception was ------- attended by representatives of both companies.
    (A) many
    (B) some
    (C) well
    (D) quite

16. The publisher is ------- located at the intersection of Seventh Avenue and Milltown Street.
    (A) convenience
    (B) convenient
    (C) inconvenient
    (D) conveniently

Part 6 Text Completion 長文穴埋め問題

英文の4つの空所を埋めるのに適切な語句を、(A) ～ (D)から選んでマークしましょう。

Questions 17-20 refer to the following letter.

Joseph Katz
85 Harden Lane

Dear Joseph,

We are pleased to inform you that you have been selected for the position of Assistant Manager. ---17--- .

Your first day of work with us will be on March 4. Please arrive at 9:00 A.M. on that day ---18--- come to the human resources department. Your supervisor, Hiro Yamamoto, ---19--- you there and show you the department. He will also help you set ---20--- a company ID and computer password. After that, he will discuss the ongoing projects in your department.

Kind regards,

Brenda Collins
Human Resources
Hailz Truck Co.

---

17. (A) We are actively discussing your application.
(B) Many people applied, but you were the best candidate.
(C) We have agreed to invest with you.
(D) A delivery schedule will be e-mailed.

18. (A) as
(B) and
(C) either
(D) for

19. (A) has met
(B) has been meeting
(C) could have met
(D) will meet

20. (A) off
(B) back
(C) up
(D) down

Part 7 Reading Comprehension 読解問題

文書を読み、5つの設問の答えとして適切なものを(A) 〜 (D)から選んでマークしましょう。

Questions 21-25 refer to the following advertisement and e-mail.

City News
EMPLOYMENT SECTION
WEDNESDAY, SEPTEMBER 21, 2016

**Office Manager Wanted, Stannor Investment Co.
Headquartered in Cape Town, South Africa**

We are looking for a candidate to take charge of our Durban branch. Manager duties will include setting business goals, making quarterly reports, and choosing suppliers. Submit your credentials to Marvin L'mumba, human resources assistant: m.lmum@stannorinv.co.za. Interviews begin on October 18.

Stannor: The Wise Investor's First Choice
www.stannorinvestment.co.za
Stocks—Bonds—Currencies—Real Estate
New offices opening in Pretoria and Johannesburg in December

E-mail

From:	Karen Plante <karen30@onemail.com>
To:	Marvin L'mumba <m.lmum@stannorinv.co.za>
Date:	September 24
Subject:	Your Open Position
Attachment:	Work history and academic records

Dear Mr. L'mumba,

I am writing regarding your opening advertised in the September 21 *City News*. I currently work for Garvey Wholesalers.

I have expert-level knowledge in the responsibilities you mentioned and supervise 50 warehouse employees. The best times to reach me on my cell phone are weekdays before 9:00 A.M. or after 6:00 P.M. or anytime on weekends.

Yours truly,

Karen Plante
Operations Manager, Garvey Wholesalers

21. According to the advertisement, where is the location of the job opening?

   (A) In Cape Town
   (B) In Durban
   (C) In Pretoria
   (D) In Johannesburg

22. Who most likely is Marvin L'mumba?

   (A) A supply manager
   (B) An online editor
   (C) An international investor
   (D) A personnel staff member

23. What does Ms. Plante state she has expertise in doing?

   (A) Writing for newspapers
   (B) Choosing stocks
   (C) Creating business targets
   (D) Recruiting employees

24. When may Ms. Plante be reached on her cell phone on Tuesdays?

   (A) At 9:30 A.M.
   (B) At noon
   (C) At 5:30 P.M.
   (D) At 8:00 P.M.

25. What has been attached to the e-mail?

   (A) A media profile
   (B) A résumé
   (C) A list of employees
   (D) Weekend work schedules

Tips for Part 7 | 2つの文書を参照して解く問題

本ユニットのようにふたつの文書が提示されているPart 7をダブル・パッセージ問題といいます。3つの文が提示されるパターン（トリプル・パッセージ問題）もあり、それらをまとめて、マルチプル・パッセージ問題と呼びます。

そのマルチプル・パッセージ問題とシングル・パッセージ問題の最大の違いは、前者の場合、2つの文書を参照しなければ解けない問題がある点です。上の問題で言うと、No. 23がそれにあたります。

ひとつの文書だけで答えが見つからない場合には、そのほかの文書にも目を通し、情報を関連付けながら、答えを探し出しましょう。

Unit 5
Meals

食事

Vocabulary Building

 A-57 ▶ A-58

次の1～15はTOEIC頻出語句です。それぞれの意味を選択肢a～oから選び答えましょう。

1. caterer　　　（名）（　　）
2. complaint　　（名）（　　）
3. coupon　　　（名）（　　）
4. delightful　　（形）（　　）
5. diner　　　　（名）（　　）
6. give away ~　　　（　　）
7. make it　　　　　（　　）
8. meal　　　　（名）（　　）
9. offer　　　　（名）（　　）
10. prefer　　　（動）（　　）
11. recipe　　　（名）（　　）
12. review　　　（名）（　　）
13. serve　　　（動）（　　）
14. stack　　　（動）（　　）
15. supervise　（動）（　　）

▶ 選択肢
- a. 調理法
- b. 批評記事、評価
- c. ～を無料で与える
- d. とても楽しい
- e. 食事
- f. ～を積み重ねる
- g. 食事をする人、食堂
- h. 申し出、割引
- i. うまくやり遂げる、間に合う
- j. クーポン、割引券
- k. 仕出し業者
- l. 不満、苦情
- m. ～の方を好む
- n. （食事など）を出す
- o. ～を監督する、管理する

Listening Section

Tips for Part 2 | 付加疑問文のコツ

苦手とする人が多い付加疑問文もPart 2で出題されます。付加疑問文といっても難しく考えず、普通の疑問文と同じように考えれば、応答で混乱せずにすみます。

> 例 You don't like spicy food, do you?
> = Do you like spicy food?

普通の疑問文と同じなので、応答のyes は「好き」、noは「好きではない」を意味します。

Training A-59

音声を聞き、質問Qへの応答を書き取りましょう。

1. Q You like Chinese food, don't you? → A _____
2. Q You've been to Seoul, haven't you? → A _____
3. Q You haven't tried Pakistani dishes, have you? → A _____
4. Q You don't like fast food, do you? → A _____

Part 1　Photographs　写真描写問題　A-60 ▶ A-61

4つの英文(A) 〜 (D)を聞き、写真を正しく描写するものを選んでマークしましょう。

1.

Ⓐ Ⓑ Ⓒ Ⓓ

2.

Part 2 Question-Response 応答問題 🎧 A-62 ▶ A-66

問いかけに対する3つの応答(A)～(C)を聞き、正しいものを選んでマークしましょう。

3. Ⓐ Ⓑ Ⓒ   4. Ⓐ Ⓑ Ⓒ   5. Ⓐ Ⓑ Ⓒ   6. Ⓐ Ⓑ Ⓒ   7. Ⓐ Ⓑ Ⓒ

Part 3 Short Conversations 会話問題 🎧 A-67 ▶ A-68

会話を聞き、3つの設問の答えとして適切なものを(A)～(D)から選んでマークしましょう。

8. Where is the restaurant?
   (A) In the shopping center
   (B) Next to Central Station
   (C) Near the office entrance
   (D) Close to the park

9. What do the waiters do at the Thai restaurant?
   (A) Bring you a tie
   (B) Carry your bags
   (C) Wear traditional clothes
   (D) Provide chopsticks

Ⓐ Ⓑ Ⓒ Ⓓ

10. What will the man probably do next?
    (A) Go back to work
    (B) Put on warm clothing
    (C) Walk to the restaurant
    (D) Turn up the air conditioning

Ⓐ Ⓑ Ⓒ Ⓓ

Part 4　Short Talks　説明文問題　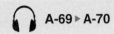

説明文を聞き、3つの設問の答えとして適切なものを(A) 〜 (D)から選んでマークしましょう。

11. What is being advertised?

(A) A gift shop
(B) A restaurant
(C) A bakery
(D) A department store

12. What did Lisa Dean do last month?

(A) She interviewed a family.
(B) She gave away coupons.
(C) She wrote an article.
(D) She judged a contest.

13. According to the speaker, what is available on the Web site?

(A) Special offers
(B) Weekly business hours
(C) Magazine comments
(D) Customer reviews

Reading Section

One Point Grammar ▶▶▶ 時制

● **1. 現在形**：事実や習慣的に行っていることを表します。

例 ① I usually **drink** coffee in the morning.
　　② He usually **skips** breakfast.

● **2. 進行形**：〈be動詞＋doing〉の形で、進行中の動作や出来事を表します。

例 ① Mr. Young **is talking** on the phone right now.
　　② Some people **were having** their meals at the table.

● **3. 過去形**：過去の事実や習慣を表します。

例 ① We **worked** late yesterday.
　　② Andy **used** to work in Jakarta.　※used to do は〈かつて～していた〉の意。

● **4. 現在完了形**：「ちょうど～した」や、出来事や経験が現在まで続いていることを表します。

例 I **have** just **ordered** a new computer online.

重要　**forとsinceのちがい**
　　I haven't seen him **for** 10 years.　　　　　　　　　　　［期間の長さ］
　　I haven't seen him **since** we graduated from college.　［いつ始まったか］

● **5. 未来のことを表す形**

例 ① The restaurant **will open** its new branch next month.
　　② I'**m having dinner** with my clients this evening.
　　③ We'**re going to visit** a gallery after having dinner.

Tips for Part 5 and 6 │ 時制のヒントとなる語句

選択肢にbecame ／ are becoming ／ will becomeなど異なる時制が並んでいる場合、文脈から正しい時制を判断します。その際、キーとなるのが、特定の時制と一緒に使われる語句です。例えばright nowなら、現在形や現在進行形とよく一緒に使われます。

（特定の時制とよく一緒に使われる語句がヒントになる！）

例 Smart phones ------- very popular right now.

ほかにも、agoは過去形、sinceやforは現在完了形などがあります。

Training

文脈から時制を判断し、(　　)の語句のうち適切なものを丸で囲みましょう。

1. They (eat / ate / have been eating) their meals for two hours.
2. Allen (visits / visited) his parents every Sunday.
3. They (know / knew / have known) each other since they were students.
4. We (started / will start / will have started) the meeting when he comes.

Part 5　Incomplete Sentences　短文穴埋め問題

英文の空所を埋めるのに適切な語句を、(A) 〜 (D)から選んでマークしましょう。

14. The first diner ------- by Scott Walter, who sold food, in 1872.

(A) created
(B) was created
(C) has created
(D) has been created

15. Creating this restaurant ------- an important step toward providing healthy menus.

(A) to be
(B) will be
(C) being
(D) have to be

16. The restaurant ------- ever since it started sharing some of their recipes.

(A) being popular
(B) were popular
(C) has been popular
(D) will have been popular

17. Liz Coleman has recently ------- positive reviews for her delicious and reasonable dishes.

(A) received
(B) receives
(C) will receive
(D) will be receiving

18. Franz Rossi ------- the kitchen at Grand Hotel for 15 years at the end of next month.

(A) is supervising
(B) has supervised
(C) has been supervising
(D) will have supervised

Part 6 Text Completion 長文穴埋め問題

英文の4つの空所を埋めるのに適切な語句を、(A)～(D)から選んでマークしましょう。

Questions 19-22 refer to the following e-mail.

To: Muhammed Abboud
From: Kelli Banks
Date: November 25
Subject: Year-end party

Muhammed,

We usually hire Chixton Caterers for our special ------- . These, of course, include our
    19.
year-end parties. They ------- good work for us in the past, but their prices are high.
          20.
------- . For this reason, I have been looking at some other options.
 21.
Skolda Catering seems ------- much lower prices. I suggest meeting with their
                 22.
representatives to see what they can do for us. Please e-mail me back with your thoughts.

Thanks,

Kelli

---

19. (A) figures
(B) events
(C) downloads
(D) collections

20. (A) are doing
(B) will do
(C) have done
(D) will have done

21. (A) Their outstanding quality is worth their high prices.
(B) Some of their reports were complex but understandable.
(C) It is only logical to remain with our current supplier.
(D) We are in a situation where we must reduce expenses.

22. (A) offer
(B) will offer
(C) offering
(D) to offer

Part 7 Reading Comprehension 読解問題

文書を読み、3つの設問の答えとして適切なものを(A)〜(D)から選んでマークしましょう。

Questions 23-25 refer to the following restaurant review.

Le Houx: Quality French Cooking
by Lisa Hellier for *Woodside Now*

The opening of Woodside's newest restaurant, Le Houx, was delayed for three months while head chef, Loic Moreau, returned to France. —[1]—. Is he worth the wait?

Woodside Now thinks so. —[2]—. We went for traditional onion soup, chicken with mushrooms and cheese, and a chocolate and orange cake. Each dish was impressive and made with food from local farms.

—[3]—. Our waiter was also excellent: helpful, polite, and able to recommend the perfect drink to match each course. The 15% service charge was worth it. —[4]—.

Our one complaint is that the restaurant is located in the middle of a residential area, and therefore difficult to get to. However, the food at Le Houx is still one of the best in Woodside.

---

23. Who most likely is Ms. Hellier?

(A) A cooking teacher
(B) A French chef
(C) A restaurant owner
(D) An article writer

Ⓐ Ⓑ Ⓒ Ⓓ

24. What is suggested about the restaurant?

(A) Its staff is rude.
(B) It is small.
(C) Its service is slow.
(D) It is not easy to visit.

Ⓐ Ⓑ Ⓒ Ⓓ

25. In which of the positions marked [1], [2], [3], and [4] does the following sentence best belong?

"Our food on Sunday evening was delightful."

(A) [1]
(B) [2]
(C) [3]
(D) [4]

Ⓐ Ⓑ Ⓒ Ⓓ

Unit 6
Communication

コミュニケーション

Vocabulary Building　　A-71 ▶ A-72

次の1〜15はTOEIC頻出語句です。それぞれの意味を選択肢a〜oから選び答えましょう。

1. as soon as possible （　　）
2. *be* supposed to *do* （　　）
3. comment （動）（　　）
4. contact （動）（　　）
5. currently （副）（　　）
6. describe （動）（　　）
7. extension （名）（　　）
8. hang up （　　）
9. in detail （　　）
10. install （動）（　　）
11. on behalf of 〜 （　　）
12. proposal （名）（　　）
13. reschedule （動）（　　）
14. respond （動）（　　）
15. voicemail （名）（　　）

▶ 選択肢

a. 現在は
b. （電話の）内線
c. 留守番電話、音声メール
d. できるだけ早く
e. 電話を切る
f. 〜の予定を変更する、延期する
g. 〜に連絡する
h. 提案、企画
i. 〜することになっている
j. 〜を設置する、導入する
k. 意見を述べる
l. 〜に代わって、代表して
m. 返答する、〜と答える
n. 詳細に
o. 〜を描写する、説明する

Listening Section

Tips for Part 2 | 会話が成立するかどうか

Part 2では、実際の会話のように、あいまいな答えや、質問に対し質問を返すやりとりも出題されます。直接的な応答がない場合も、自然な会話の流れになる応答を選びます。

例 Is there a cafeteria in this building?

→ Are you new here?

会話が成立するかどうかを重視する！

この例の応答は、質問に質問を返す形ですが、会話が成立しているので正答です。

Training　　A-73

自然な応答になるよう線で結びましょう。答えは音声で確認してください。

1. Where is the new theater?
2. I want to use a calculator.
3. This is the most interesting job I've ever had.
4. Who's working on the new project?

a. Miles might have one.
b. Probably Kathy knows who is.
c. Where did you work before this?
d. I can show you the way.

Part 1　Photographs　写真描写問題　A-74 ▶ A-75

4つの英文(A)〜(D)を聞き、写真を正しく描写するものを選んでマークしましょう。

1.

Ⓐ Ⓑ Ⓒ Ⓓ

2. 　Ⓐ Ⓑ Ⓒ Ⓓ

Part 2　Question-Response　応答問題　🎧 A-76 ▶ A-80

問いかけに対する3つの応答(A)〜(C)を聞き、正しいものを選んでマークしましょう。

3. Ⓐ Ⓑ Ⓒ　　4. Ⓐ Ⓑ Ⓒ　　5. Ⓐ Ⓑ Ⓒ　　6. Ⓐ Ⓑ Ⓒ　　7. Ⓐ Ⓑ Ⓒ

Part 3　Short Conversations　会話問題　🎧 A-81 ▶ A-82

会話を聞き、3つの設問の答えとして適切なものを(A)〜(D)から選んでマークしましょう。

8. Why is the man calling?
   (A) To reschedule an event
   (B) To order some products
   (C) To respond to a question
   (D) To update an account

   Ⓐ Ⓑ Ⓒ Ⓓ

9. Who most likely is Ms. Lin?
   (A) An athlete
   (B) A company supervisor
   (C) A receptionist
   (D) A tour guide

   Ⓐ Ⓑ Ⓒ Ⓓ

10. What is Ms. Lin supposed to do on March 8?
    (A) Confirm a message
    (B) Change suppliers
    (C) Send factory supplies
    (D) Visit a facility

    Ⓐ Ⓑ Ⓒ Ⓓ

Part 4 — Short Talks 説明文問題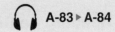

説明文を聞き、3つの設問の答えとして適切なものを(A)～(D)から選んでマークしましょう。

11. Why would a caller hear this message?

    (A) All of the voicemail boxes are full.
    (B) The offices are currently closed.
    (C) The phone number has been changed.
    (D) All of the lines are busy.

12. What are callers with urgent problems asked to do?

    (A) Call a different number
    (B) Describe their emergencies
    (C) Come to the clinic
    (D) Leave a special message

13. Why would a caller press 1?

    (A) To enter an extension
    (B) To find a staff member
    (C) To leave information
    (D) To hear the message again

Reading Section

One Point Grammar ▶▶▶ 受動態・分詞

● 1. 受動態の形：受動態は〈be動詞＋過去分詞〉で「～される」を表します。

例 ① Mr. James **is** well **known** as the host of a popular TV show.
② The house **was damaged** by the storm.
③ The agenda needs to **be reviewed** as soon as possible.

● 2. 受動態の時制：受動態はさまざまな時制と組み合わせて使われます。

例 ① Their new product **is being advertised** on TV now.
② A copying machine **has been placed** next to the staff lounge.
③ The annual conference **will be held** at Richmond Hotel.

● 3. 注意すべき使い方

〔1〕感情を表現する場合

例 ① I **was surprised** at the news.　　　　　　　　　［×］was surprising
② Ms. Stanley **is interested** in applying for the managing position.
　　　　　　　　　　　　　　　　　　　　　　　　　　　［×］is interesting

〔2〕-ed形が形容詞の役割をする場合

例 ① The forecast is based on the annual survey **conducted** by the department.
② Mr. Cooper is an **experienced** consultant.

〔3〕まちがいやすい表現

例 ① The flight **was delayed** due to bad weather.　　［×］The flight delayed
② Kelly **was dressed** in black.　　　　　　　　　　　［×］Kelly dressed
③ Mr. & Mrs. Clark **have been married** for 10 years.　［×］have married

---

Tips for Part 5 and 6 │ 主語は人かモノか

感情を表現する場合、主語が人の場合は-ed形、主語がモノ・出来事などの場合は-ing形と覚えておきましょう。次の空所には、excitedとexcitingのどちらが入りますか。

〈主語が人（I）なので、-ed形が入る。〉

例 I was really ------- because the movie was really thrilling.

excitedは「人がわくわくしている」、excitingは「モノ・出来事がわくわくさせるような」を表すので、excitedが適切です。

Training

( )の語句のうち適切なものを丸で囲みましょう。

1. I'm (interesting / interested) in the position, but I do not have much experience.
2. After working long hours, the staff felt (exhausting / exhausted).
3. The (dissatisfying / dissatisfied) customer wanted to request a refund.
4. Every photograph at the gallery was very (fascinating / fascinated) to look at.
5. What (surprising / surprised) trend was mentioned in the report?

Part 5 Incomplete Sentences 短文穴埋め問題

英文の空所を埋めるのに適切な語句を、(A)～(D)から選んでマークしましょう。

14. The award ------- by the Scholar Foundation once a year.
(A) gives
(B) gave
(C) is given
(D) have given

15. Customers are ------- to contact our staff for any questions or complaints.
(A) encouraged
(B) encourage
(C) encourages
(D) encouraging

16. The procedure will be ------- in detail in the next meeting.
(A) explain
(B) explains
(C) explained
(D) to explain

17. The employees were ------- to learn that they would receive a big bonus.
(A) excitement
(B) excitedly
(C) exciting
(D) excited

18. The banquet originally planned for this Friday will be ------- until next Thursday.
(A) awarded
(B) postponed
(C) complained
(D) described

Part 6 Text Completion 長文穴埋め問題

英文の4つの空所を埋めるのに適切な語句を、(A)〜(D)から選んでマークしましょう。

Questions 19-22 refer to the following e-mail.

To: All employees
From: Lakshmi Chopra
Date: December 17
Subject: Software system

Dear Staff,

------- . As a result, we have chosen a new, companywide system. We ------- it on
  19.   **20.**
Wednesday, December 21, from 6:00 A.M. to 7:30 A.M. We have chosen this time since
it should have the ------- impact on staff.
                     21.

If you plan on coming in during that ------- , remember that you will not be able to access
                                             22.
the company system.

Regards,

Lakshmi Chopra
IT Manager

---

19. (A) We need your ideas on a solution.
    (B) Our systems clearly need improvement.
    (C) The computers are still powerful enough for us.
    (D) All staff who buy the app will receive a discount.
                       Ⓐ Ⓑ Ⓒ Ⓓ

20. (A) will install
    (B) installing
    (C) are installed
    (D) being installed
                       Ⓐ Ⓑ Ⓒ Ⓓ

21. (A) more or less
    (B) less
    (C) least
    (D) much less
                       Ⓐ Ⓑ Ⓒ Ⓓ

22. (A) broadcast
    (B) trial
    (C) period
    (D) conference
                       Ⓐ Ⓑ Ⓒ Ⓓ

Tips for Part 7 │ イントロがヒントになる

Part 7だけでなく、Part 4もそうですが、問題の冒頭に書かれている（読まれる）イントロが解答の助けになります。事前にパッセージの種類がわかるからです。

　　　　　　　　これから読む文章が「記事」だと分かる。

例 **Questions 153-155 refer to the following article.**

068 │ Unit 6

Part 7 Reading Comprehension 読解問題

文書を読み、3つの設問の答えとして適切なものを(A) ～ (D)から選んでマークしましょう。

Questions 23-25 refer to the following telephone message.

To: **Jasmine Wright**

Caller: **Samuel Goldstein**

Message taken by: **Piotr Stepanovich**

Date: **May 13**   Time of Call: **11:30 A.M.**

Message:

Samuel Goldstein said he will be busy with new conferences with other suppliers on the morning of May 15 and won't be free until 2:00 P.M. Therefore, he would like you to visit his office at that time instead of 1:00 P.M. on that day. You can show him your proposals at that time. He'd like you to respond by noon to confirm whether this is okay. He said you had his contact information.

Piotr

---

23. Who most likely is Samuel Goldstein?

(A) A coworker
(B) A supplier
(C) A customer
(D) A supervisor

Ⓐ Ⓑ Ⓒ Ⓓ

24. According to the message, why does Mr. Goldstein want a change?

(A) To use a different office
(B) To complete prior meetings
(C) To visit on a different day
(D) To introduce more proposals

Ⓐ Ⓑ Ⓒ Ⓓ

25. When is the earliest Ms. Wright may visit Mr. Goldstein on May 15?

(A) At 11:30 A.M.
(B) At 12:00 noon
(C) At 1:00 P.M.
(D) At 2:00 P.M.

Ⓐ Ⓑ Ⓒ Ⓓ

Unit 7
Fun

楽しみ

Vocabulary Building B-02 ▶ B-03

次の1〜15はTOEIC頻出語句です。それぞれの意味を選択肢a〜oから選び答えましょう。

1. attraction　　（名）（　　）
2. enclosed　　（形）（　　）
3. feature　　（動）（　　）
4. fill out 〜　　　　（　　）
5. hesitate　　（動）（　　）
6. include　　（動）（　　）
7. indicate　　（動）（　　）
8. instrument　　（名）（　　）
9. launch　　（動）（　　）
10. performance　　（名）（　　）
11. questionnaire　　（名）（　　）
12. subscribe to 〜　　（　　）
13. suggestion　　（名）（　　）
14. suitable　　（形）（　　）
15. upcoming　　（形）（　　）

▶ 選択肢
a. 呼び物
b. 次の、やって来る
c. 〜を示す
d. 〜を含む
e. ためらう
f. アンケート
g. 〜を定期購読する
h. 公演、演奏
i. 〜を売り出す、開始する
j. 器具、楽器
k. 提案
l. 適切な、ふさわしい
m. 〜に記入する
n. 同封の
o. 〜を特集する、〜を（大きく）扱う

Listening Section

Tips for Part 2 ｜ 提案・勧誘・依頼の表現

Part 2 では、さまざまな提案や勧誘、依頼の表現が登場します。例えば、Why don't we ... ?と聞こえてくれば「何かをしようと提案している」と瞬間的に意味が浮かぶよう、頻出表現を覚えましょう。応答パターンと一緒に覚えることが大切です。

定型表現に慣れる

例 **Why don't we take a taxi to the station?**

[肯定] Sounds like a good idea.
[否定] We might be caught in a traffic jam.

Training B-04

自然な応答を線で結びましょう。答えは音声で確認してください。

1. May I use this computer?   •   • a. I'd rather you didn't.
2. Would you like something to eat?   •   • b. That's something I need.
3. Why don't you take a day off?   •   • c. Sure, go ahead.
4. Do you mind if I smoke?   •   • d. No, thank you. I'm full.

Part 1 Photographs 写真描写問題   B-05 ▶ B-06

4つの英文(A)〜(D)を聞き、写真を正しく描写するものを選んでマークしましょう。

1.

Ⓐ Ⓑ Ⓒ Ⓓ

2.

Part 2 Question-Response 応答問題   🎧 B-07 ▶ B-11

問いかけに対する3つの応答(A)～(C)を聞き、正しいものを選んでマークしましょう。

3. Ⓐ Ⓑ Ⓒ   4. Ⓐ Ⓑ Ⓒ   5. Ⓐ Ⓑ Ⓒ   6. Ⓐ Ⓑ Ⓒ   7. Ⓐ Ⓑ Ⓒ

Part 3 Short Conversations 会話問題   🎧 B-12 ▶ B-13

会話を聞き、3つの設問の答えとして適切なものを(A)～(D)から選んでマークしましょう。

8. What does the man say about Yuko?
   (A) She worked in a different department.
   (B) She posted a musical review.
   (C) She had extra tickets.
   (D) She liked a performance.

9. Why does the man say, "Sounds great"?
   (A) He has a really good idea.
   (B) He expects great results.
   (C) He appreciates another person.
   (D) He welcomes a suggestion.

10. What do the women suggest?
    (A) Departing soon
    (B) Leaving a complaint
    (C) Choosing an office space
    (D) Paying a parking lot fee

Part 4　Short Talks　説明文問題　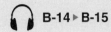

説明文を聞き、3つの設問の答えとして適切なものを(A)〜(D)から選んでマークしましょう。

Central Museum
Special Exhibits

- **Black and White Photography**
- **Egyptian Masks**
- **Ancient Coins** (New this month)
- **Russian Art** (Coming soon)

---

11. Look at the graphic. What exhibit will the listeners see?

(A) Black and White Photography
(B) Egyptian Masks
(C) Ancient Coins
(D) Russian Art

Ⓐ Ⓑ Ⓒ Ⓓ

12. According to the speaker, how long will the tour take?

(A) One hour
(B) Two hours
(C) Three hours
(D) Four hours

Ⓐ Ⓑ Ⓒ Ⓓ

13. What are the listeners invited to do?

(A) Buy special gifts
(B) Ask any questions
(C) Wait for lunch to end
(D) Pick up free booklets

Ⓐ Ⓑ Ⓒ Ⓓ

Reading Section

One Point Grammar ▶▶▶ 動名詞と不定詞

● 1. 動名詞

動詞の語尾に -ing をつけて「～すること」と名詞のように使います。

例 ① I have to finish **editing** the article by tomorrow morning.
② He should give up **smoking**.

● 2. 不定詞

動詞（原形）の前に to をつけた to do の形で使います。

例 ① The board has asked Dr. Ting **to lead** the research team.　［名詞的用法］
② Could you get something **to eat** for us?　［形容詞的用法］
③ Flight 245 is not yet ready **to receive** passengers.　［副詞的用法］

● 3. 注意すべき使い方

〔1〕動名詞のみ、不定詞のみを続ける動詞

動名詞のみを続ける動詞	avoid, consider, deny, enjoy, finish, keep, mind, postpone, practice, risk, suggest
不定詞のみを続ける動詞	afford, agree, appear, decide, fail, hesitate, hope, learn, manage, plan, pretend, promise, refuse, seem, tend, want

〔2〕動名詞と不定詞で意味が変わる動詞。

例 ① He **stopped** smoking. ／ He **stopped** to smoke.
② I **forgot** closing the window. ／ Don't **forget** to close the window.

重要　前置詞の to には動名詞（-ing形）が続く
① I'm looking forward to **talking** with you soon.　［×］to talk
② They are opposed to **shopping** online.　［×］to shop
③ I get used to **living** in this town.　［×］to live

Tips for Part 5 and 6 ｜ 動名詞 vs. 不定詞

動名詞（-ing形）のみ、あるいは to 不定詞のみが続く動詞はかぎられています。整理しておきましょう。次の例文には、mentioning と to discuss、どちらが入るでしょうか。

後ろに動名詞と to 不定詞どちらが続く単語か把握しておく

例 ① They avoided ------- the problem.
② They decided ------- the problem.

avoid は動名詞、decide は to 不定詞を続ける動詞なので、①に mentioning、②に to discuss が入りますね。

Training

[　] 内の動詞を適切な形に直して、文を完成させましょう。

1. Mr. Dean managed _____ the deadline. [meet]
2. Visitors are not allowed _____ pictures inside the building. [take]
3. I'm seriously considering _____ a musical instrument. [learn]
4. Do you mind _____ the door for me? [hold]

Part 5　Incomplete Sentences　短文穴埋め問題

英文の空所を埋めるのに適切な語句を、(A) ～ (D) から選んでマークしましょう。

14. According to a survey, younger generations enjoy ------- home.
 (A) staying
 (B) to stay
 (C) stay
 (D) stayed

15. The institution made their staff ------- to the monthly journal.
 (A) subscribe
 (B) subscribing
 (C) to subscribe
 (D) be subscribed

16. Fliers for the upcoming performance are ready to ------- to visitors to the theater.
 (A) distribute
 (B) be distributing
 (C) be distributed
 (D) have distributed

17. Some parts of the museum need ------- before the international exhibition.
 (A) restoring
 (B) to restore
 (C) restored
 (D) restore

18. Please do not ------- to ask the receptionist if you need additional information.
 (A) finish
 (B) deny
 (C) manage
 (D) hesitate

Part 6 Text Completion 長文穴埋め問題

英文の4つの空所を埋めるのに適切な語句を、(A) ～ (D)から選んでマークしましょう。

Questions 19-22 refer to the following article.

(January 17) The Ressfeld Museum was finally launched yesterday. ------- . There
                                                                    19.
were long visitor lines outside even before its grand ------- . The museum
                                                      20.
welcomed over 10,000 visitors on its first day of business. It expects even more

people ------- . All guests appeared well-satisfied with their ------- . Entrance is
       21.   **22.**
$8.75 for adults and $5.00 for students under 18. Children under five can enter

free.

---

19. (A) It quickly became a very popular attraction.
　　　 (B) Our town is finally building some new schools.
　　　 (C) Artworks will be sold to the highest bidders.
　　　 (D) It is much easier than finding new experts.
　　　　　　　　　　　　　　　Ⓐ Ⓑ Ⓒ Ⓓ

20. (A) to open
　　　 (B) opening
　　　 (C) will open
　　　 (D) had opened
　　　　　　　　　　　　　　　Ⓐ Ⓑ Ⓒ Ⓓ

21. (A) casually
　　　 (B) thankfully
　　　 (C) daily
　　　 (D) responsively
　　　　　　　　　　　　　　　Ⓐ Ⓑ Ⓒ Ⓓ

22. (A) invention
　　　 (B) allowance
　　　 (C) experience
　　　 (D) supervisor
　　　　　　　　　　　　　　　Ⓐ Ⓑ Ⓒ Ⓓ

076 | Unit 7

Part 7 Reading Comprehension 読解問題

文書を読み、3つの設問の答えとして適切なものを(A)〜(D)から選んでマークしましょう。

Questions 23-25 refer to the following letter.

Dear Ms. Turner:

Please find enclosed four tickets for our Christmas entertainment at historic Bramble Castle. The main show will feature performances from jugglers and musicians. Your children will enjoy watching amazing card tricks and looking for presents hidden around the castle. Every child will be able to collect a suitable gift from Santa. Adults will enjoy watching an exhibition of historic musical instruments in the castle's museum.

Looking forward to your visit.

Sinita Patel

Sinita Patel
Manager, Bramble Castle

---

23. What is this letter about?
    (A) A rock concert
    (B) A feature movie
    (C) A visit to a castle
    (D) A circus

24. How many tickets are included with the letter?
    (A) One
    (B) Two
    (C) Three
    (D) Four

25. What will children enjoy?
    (A) Doing card tricks
    (B) Hiding in various places
    (C) Looking at instruments
    (D) Searching for gifts

Unit 8
Office Work

オフィスワーク

Vocabulary Building

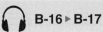

次の1～15はTOEIC頻出語句です。それぞれの意味を選択肢a～oから選び答えましょう。

1. board （名）（　　）
2. certainly （副）（　　）
3. form （名）（　　）
4. maintain （動）（　　）
5. office supplies （　　）
6. on duty （　　）
7. performance （名）（　　）
8. photocopier （名）（　　）
9. president （名）（　　）
10. promote （動）（　　）
11. relocate （動）（　　）
12. renovation （名）（　　）
13. replace （動）（　　）
14. uniform （名）（　　）
15. update （名）（　　）

▶ 選択肢
a. 事務用品、筆記用具
b. ～を昇進させる
c. 勤務時間中で
d. 最新情報
e. 改築、刷新
f. ～を取り替える
g. ～を移転させる
h. コピー機
i. 業績、成績
j. 確かに、ほんとうに
k. 社長
l. 書式、用紙
m. ～を維持する、保つ
n. 取締役会
o. 制服

Listening Section

Tips for Part 3 and 4 | 設問先読み

Part 3と4（会話問題 & 説明文問題）において、設問は貴重なヒントです。何に焦点をあてて、音声を聞けばよいかを教えてくれます。放送英文が流れる前に設問に目を通す「設問先読み」を行い、焦点をしぼった聞き取りをしましょう。

例 What will happen on <u>June 16</u>?
　 <u>Where</u> will the event take place?

- 6月16日に関する情報に集中して聞くことができる
- 「イベントがどこで」に集中して聞くことができる

Training　　　　B-18

設問を読んでから会話音声を聞き、答えを書き出しましょう。

1. Where does this conversation take place?　→ ＿＿＿＿＿＿＿＿＿＿
2. What is the woman asking about?　→ ＿＿＿＿＿＿＿＿＿＿

Part 1　Photographs　写真描写問題　B-19 ▶ B-20

4つの英文(A) 〜 (D)を聞き、写真を正しく描写するものを選んでマークしましょう。

1.

Ⓐ Ⓑ Ⓒ Ⓓ

2.

Ⓐ Ⓑ Ⓒ Ⓓ

Part 2　Question-Response　応答問題　🎧 B-21 ▶ B-24

問いかけに対する3つの応答(A)～(C)を聞き、正しいものを選んでマークしましょう。

3. Ⓐ Ⓑ Ⓒ　　**4.** Ⓐ Ⓑ Ⓒ　　**5.** Ⓐ Ⓑ Ⓒ　　**6.** Ⓐ Ⓑ Ⓒ

Part 3　Short Conversations　会話問題　🎧 B-25 ▶ B-26

会話を聞き、3つの設問の答えとして適切なものを(A)～(D)から選んでマークしましょう。

7. Why does the man ask for assistance?

(A) A project has been changed.
(B) A device is not working.
(C) A warranty has expired.
(D) A service has been canceled.

Ⓐ Ⓑ Ⓒ Ⓓ

8. What has Carmen promised to do?

(A) Fix an item
(B) Copy some documents
(C) Order more parts
(D) Inform the woman of a situation

Ⓐ Ⓑ Ⓒ Ⓓ

9. What does the man plan to do this afternoon?

(A) Buy a present
(B) Give a talk
(C) Send a fax
(D) Fill out some forms

Ⓐ Ⓑ Ⓒ Ⓓ

Part 4 Short Talks 説明文問題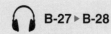

説明文を聞き、3つの設問の答えとして適切なものを(A)〜(D)から選んでマークしましょう。

10. What does the announcement say will happen on June 16?

(A) Software will be upgraded.
(B) Renovations will be launched.
(C) A new facility will be opened.
(D) A store will be closed.

Ⓐ Ⓑ Ⓒ Ⓓ

11. What is said about security personnel?

(A) They may block some areas.
(B) They will help employees relocate.
(C) They will be shifted to another place.
(D) They will guard the work crews.

Ⓐ Ⓑ Ⓒ Ⓓ

12. When will updates be posted?

(A) Every day
(B) Every other day
(C) Every week
(D) Every month

Ⓐ Ⓑ Ⓒ Ⓓ

Reading Section

One Point Grammar ▶▶▶ 助動詞

● **1. can**

This seminar **can** help you find new markets.

● **2. may**

① The best way is to e-mail me, but you **may** also call me.
② We **may** not meet the sales target this year.

● **3. might**

The CEO's scandal **might** damage the reputation of the company.

● **4. must**

① You **must** sign up for the seminar in advance.
② Ben has been working too hard this week. He **must** be tired.

● 5. should

① You **should** carefully evaluate the financial risks before starting business.
② This work **shouldn't** take so long to complete.

Tips for Part 5 and 6 | 助動詞のあとには動詞の原形

助動詞が関係した問題では、「助動詞のあとには動詞の原形が続く」がポイントとなります。
次の空所には、extendとextendedのどちらが入りますか。

> 空所から離れた位置にある助動詞を見逃さない。

例 They can easily ------- the free trial period.

easilyという副詞が間に入っていますが、助動詞canがあるので、extendが適切です。

Part 5 Incomplete Sentences 短文穴埋め問題

英文の空所を埋めるのに適切な語句を、(A) 〜 (D)から選んでマークしましょう。

13. Employees must ------- protective clothes in this laboratory.

   (A) wears
   (B) to wear
   (C) be worn
   (D) wear

14. Ms. Peters will probably ------ Bob as head of the team.

   (A) replace
   (B) replacing
   (C) replaced
   (D) be replaced

15. Our branch office in the U.K. ------- relocated from Manchester to Nottingham.

   (A) will
   (B) have
   (C) has been
   (D) have to

16. I would really appreciate it if you ------- the date of a meeting by Tuesday.

   (A) setting
   (B) have set
   (C) could be set
   (D) could set

Part 6 Text Completion 長文穴埋め問題

英文の4つの空所を埋めるのに適切な語句を、(A)〜(D)から選んでマークしましょう。

Questions 17-20 refer to the following notice.

Office Update

Kelino Plastics

We provide a company lounge for all of our employees. It is up to you to help maintain it. ------- . After finishing your meal, please clear all plates, cups, and utensils from the table. Then, wipe down the tables, ------- possible. It only takes a moment to do your ------- .
        17.   18.   19.

By doing these small things, you help us maintain this important ------- for everyone.
                                                                    20.
Thank you for your cooperation.

---

17. (A) You can submit your application to any manager.
(B) Please remember that there are no wait staff in this area.
(C) Speak to a supervisor about applying for a transfer.
(D) The launch of the product will take place on September 9.

Ⓐ Ⓑ Ⓒ Ⓓ

18. (A) whomever
(B) whatever
(C) whenever
(D) whichever

Ⓐ Ⓑ Ⓒ Ⓓ

19. (A) part
(B) calculation
(C) revision
(D) enforcement

Ⓐ Ⓑ Ⓒ Ⓓ

20. (A) supplier
(B) place
(C) currency
(D) law

Ⓐ Ⓑ Ⓒ Ⓓ

Tips for Part 7 | 受取人と差出人をチェック

毎回、必ず出題されるパッセージ形式に「手紙」、「Eメール」があります。これらの形式では、何よりもまず、誰から誰に宛てた文書なのかをチェックしてください。手紙の場合は冒頭に左寄せで宛名（役職や会社名も）が記され、末尾に差出人が記されています。Eメールの場合はアドレス部分のFrom、Toから差出人と受取人をすぐに把握できます。

Part 7 Reading Comprehension 読解問題

文書を読み、5つの設問の答えとして適切なものを(A)〜(D)から選んでマークしましょう。

Questions 21-25 refer to the following e-mails.

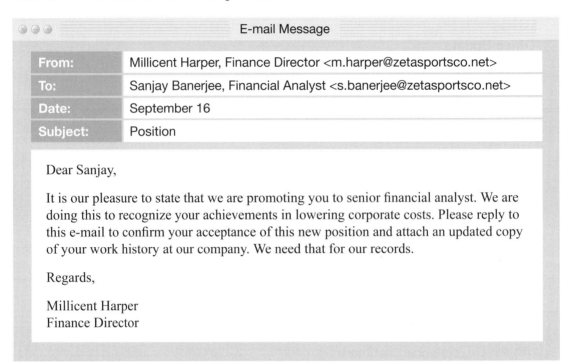

E-mail Message

From:	Millicent Harper, Finance Director <m.harper@zetasportsco.net>
To:	Sanjay Banerjee, Financial Analyst <s.banerjee@zetasportsco.net>
Date:	September 16
Subject:	Position

Dear Sanjay,

It is our pleasure to state that we are promoting you to senior financial analyst. We are doing this to recognize your achievements in lowering corporate costs. Please reply to this e-mail to confirm your acceptance of this new position and attach an updated copy of your work history at our company. We need that for our records.

Regards,

Millicent Harper
Finance Director

* E-mail *

From:	Sanjay Banerjee, Financial Analyst <s.banerjee@zetasportsco.net>
To:	Millicent Harper, Finance Director <m.harper@zetasportsco.net>
Date:	September 17
Subject:	RE: Position

Dear Ms. Harper,

I was very pleasantly surprised by your decision and accept the new job. I will do my best to fulfill its requirements. By September 19, I'll send you the information that you requested in your September 16 e-mail. Incidentally, I hope you have had a chance to look over my spreadsheets I put on your desk. They include some ideas on next year's budget.

Yours truly,

Sanjay Banerjee

21. What is the main purpose of the first e-mail?

(A) To provide a recommendation
(B) To ask about a procedure
(C) To explain a new opening
(D) To announce a change

22. According to the first e-mail, what is indicated about Mr. Banerjee?

(A) He promoted some staff members.
(B) He reduced company expenses.
(C) He updated some delivery records.
(D) He recognized a colleague's performance.

23. Why does Mr. Banerjee state he is surprised?

(A) His decision was accepted.
(B) A selection was unexpected.
(C) Some information was missing.
(D) A request was not fulfilled.

24. What will Mr. Banerjee send by September 19?

(A) Personal credentials
(B) An e-mail list
(C) Desk designs
(D) Financial spreadsheets

25. What does Mr. Banerjee state he has already done?

(A) Offered someone a position
(B) Revised job requirements
(C) Submitted some figures
(D) Increased a budget

Unit 9
Meeting

会議

Vocabulary Building 🎧 B-29 ▶ B-30

次の1〜15はTOEIC頻出語句です。それぞれの意味を選択肢a〜oから選び答えましょう。

1. address　　　（動）（　　）
2. agenda　　　（名）（　　）
3. attend　　　（動）（　　）
4. chair　　　（動）（　　）
5. competitive　（形）（　　）
6. conference　（名）（　　）
7. decline　　　（動）（　　）
8. ensure　　　（動）（　　）
9. industry　　（名）（　　）
10. outlet　　　（名）（　　）
11. profit　　　（名）（　　）
12. strategy　　（名）（　　）
13. take place　　　（　　）
14. venue　　　（名）（　　）
15. workshop　　（名）（　　）

▶ 選択肢
a. 研修会
b. 〜を保証する、確実にする
c. 〜に演説する／〜に取り組む
d. 会議、協議会
e. 〜の議長を務める
f. コンセント
g. 業界
h. 衰える、減少する
i. 起こる、行われる
j. 戦略
k. 競争力のある
l. 議題
m. 開催地、会場
n. 〜に出席する
o. 利益

Listening Section

Tips for Part 3 and 4 | 全体を問う設問

Part 3 と 4 の設問は「全体を問う設問」と「部分を問う設問」に大別できます（Part 7 も同じ）。「全体を問う設問」とは、話の大枠を尋ねる問題です。会話や放送の場所、目的やテーマ、話し手・聞き手が誰なのかが問われます。

例 Where is this announcement being made?
What are they mainly talking about?
Who is the speaker?

場所や、話し手・聞き手を理解するには、check in[out]、rooms facing the water などはホテル、departure gate、baggage claim tag は空港というように、場所や職業に特有の定番表現を覚えましょう。

Training B-31 ▶ B-34

1 ～ 4 の音声を聞き、誰と誰が話しているか、A ～ D から選びましょう。

1. (　　)　　2. (　　)　　3. (　　)　　4. (　　)

選択肢　A. a hotel guest and a clerk　　B. a shop clerk and a customer
　　　　C. colleagues　　　　　　　　　D. a customer and a travel agent

Part 1　Photographs　写真描写問題 B-35 ▶ B-36

4つの英文(A) ～ (D)を聞き、写真を正しく描写するものを選んでマークしましょう。

1.

Ⓐ Ⓑ Ⓒ Ⓓ

Meeting　会議 | 087

2.

Ⓐ Ⓑ Ⓒ Ⓓ

Part 2 Question-Response 応答問題 🎧 B-37 ▶ B-41

問いかけに対する3つの応答(A) 〜 (C)を聞き、正しいものを選んでマークしましょう。

3. Ⓐ Ⓑ Ⓒ   4. Ⓐ Ⓑ Ⓒ   5. Ⓐ Ⓑ Ⓒ   6. Ⓐ Ⓑ Ⓒ   7. Ⓐ Ⓑ Ⓒ

Part 3 Short Conversations 会話問題 🎧 B-42 ▶ B-43

会話を聞き、3つの設問の答えとして適切なものを(A) 〜 (D)から選んでマークしましょう。

8. When does this conversation take place?
   (A) Before a product launch
   (B) During a flight
   (C) After the campaign is over
   (D) Before a business meeting

Ⓐ Ⓑ Ⓒ Ⓓ

9. What does the man say about the new product?
   (A) It is expensive.
   (B) It is selling poorly.
   (C) It received good reviews.
   (D) It is easy to use.

Ⓐ Ⓑ Ⓒ Ⓓ

10. What will the speakers most likely do?
    (A) Talk about sales strategy
    (B) Launch a new Web site.
    (C) Campaign for workers' rights
    (D) Put the product on sale

Ⓐ Ⓑ Ⓒ Ⓓ

Part 4　Short Talks　説明文問題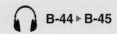

説明文を聞き、3つの設問の答えとして適切なものを(A)〜(D)から選んでマークしましょう。

11. What will Ms.Gate talk about?

(A) Her company's profits
(B) Names and addresses
(C) An industry's condition
(D) State-run companies

Ⓐ Ⓑ Ⓒ Ⓓ

12. What is happening today?

(A) Most companies are making money.
(B) Debt is rising sharply.
(C) The industry is declining.
(D) The speaker is enjoying herself.

Ⓐ Ⓑ Ⓒ Ⓓ

13. What does Ms.Gate want leaders to do?

(A) Meet her more often
(B) Take part in discussions
(C) Cancel the convention
(D) Compete with each other

Ⓐ Ⓑ Ⓒ Ⓓ

Reading Section

One Point Grammar ▶▶▶ 比較

● **1. AはBと同じくらい〜だ**

〈as＋原級＋as〉

例　Repairing the old fax machine costs **as much as** buying a new one.

● **2. AはBよりも〜だ**

〈比較級＋than〉

例　① This new type of battery lasts much **longer than** the previous type.
　　② Mr. Brown takes his job **more seriously than** his colleagues do.

※thanの代わりにtoを使う比較に注意
(1) 語尾が-iorの形容詞（superior, inferior, senior, juniorなど）
(2) prefer A to B

● 3. Aはもっとも〜だ

〈the most〉〈the＋最上級〉

例 ① VieTry has been one of **the most** successful businesses in Vietnam.
② Ms. Smith always works (the) **hardest** in the office.

● 4. 重要な表現

〔1〕〈as＋原級＋as possible〉 「できるだけ〜」
〔2〕 no later than ... 「…までに」
〔3〕〈the＋比較級, the＋比較級〉 「〜すればするほど…」

例 ① Please send your payment **as soon as possible**.
② Fax your estimate to us **no later than** May 31.
③ **The more** people earn, **the more** they spend.

重要　不規則に変化する語を覚えよう

原級	比較級	最上級
good/well	better	best
bad	worse	worst
little	less	least
many/much	more	most

Tips for Part 5 and 6 ｜ 比較のヒント

原級・比較級・最上級の判断を下すには、次の点をヒントとします。①「AはBと同じくらい〜」は、空所前後にas (so)があるか、②「AはBより〜だ」はthanがあるか、③「Aはもっとも〜だ」は冠詞theがあるか。次の文にそれぞれeasyとdifficultを適切に変化させ空所に入れてみましょう。

これらをヒントに判断を下す！

例 This question is <u>as</u> ------- as that question.
This question is ------- <u>than</u> that question.
This question is one of <u>the</u> ------- questions in this book.

Training

( ) 内の語句のうち、適切なものを丸で囲みましょう。

1. Tickets were (fewer / less) expensive than we expected.
2. Your presentation was one of the (more / most) convincing ones I've ever heard.
3. We have (more / most) meetings this year compared with last year.
4. The more studying you do now, the (easier / easiest) the test will be.

Part 5 Incomplete Sentences 短文穴埋め問題

英文の空所を埋めるのに適切な語句を、(A) 〜 (D)から選んでマークしましょう。

14. The meeting will start half an hour ------- than usual today.
(A) late
(B) later
(C) latest
(D) lateness

15. The members tried to address the problem as ------- as possible.
(A) effect
(B) effective
(C) effectively
(D) more effective

16. The seminar was attended by ------- employees compared with the previous one.
(A) more
(B) very
(C) most
(D) much

17. Polar Hotel is preferred ------- the Convention Center as a meeting place.
(A) more
(B) over
(C) with
(D) for

18. The venue for the conference is ------- visited by train than the site we used last year.
(A) easier
(B) easiest
(C) more easily
(D) most easily

Part 6 Text Completion 長文穴埋め問題

英文の4つの空所を埋めるのに適切な語句を、(A)～(D)から選んでマークしましょう。

Questions 19-22 refer to the following e-mail.

To: Department managers
From: Valeria Lopez
Date: May 2
Subject: Upcoming Meeting

Dear All,

Tomorrow's meeting was ------- scheduled for 10:30 A.M. in Room 16D.
             19.

That room is quite spacious but since it -------, we will be holding the meeting in
                                         20.
Room 24C instead. This room is ------- than the other, but still has enough space.
                                21.
Please feel free to bring your laptops to the room. -------.
                                                    22.

I've already e-mailed you the agenda that you will need.

Thanks,

Valeria Lopez
Division Manager

---

19. (A) originate
(B) origin
(C) original
(D) originally

20. (A) is being painted
(B) will be painting
(C) to be painted
(D) has painted

21. (A) small
(B) very small
(C) much smaller
(D) the smallest

22. (A) Contact a service representative with any complaints.
(B) We guarantee all of our items for 18 months.
(C) Most of the machinery is ready for production.
(D) There are many electrical outlets that you can use.

Part 7 Reading Comprehension 読解問題

文書を読み、3つの設問の答えとして適切なものを(A)〜(D)から選んでマークしましょう。

Questions 23-25 refer to the following schedule.

Saturday Workshop for Administration
Schedule

10:00 A.M. — 12:00 noon	*Don't rush! Better Timekeeping as the Key to Success*
	Lunch
1:00 P.M. — 3:00 P.M.	*Choosing the Right Venue for Your Conference*
	Break
3:30 P.M. — 5:30 P.M.	*Communicating Goals to Your Workforce with a Clear Presentation*
	Break
5:45 P.M. — 6:00 P.M.	*Closing Remarks*

We would like to point out that any managers wishing to attend this workshop should register with the head office in advance and then check in at the reception desk on the day.

---

23. Who is this conference for?
  (A) Secretaries
  (B) Manual workers
  (C) Management
  (D) Temporary staff

24. When does the workshop for time management start?
  (A) 10:00 A.M.
  (B) 1:00 P.M.
  (C) 3:30 P.M.
  (D) 5:45 P.M.

25. What should readers do first if they want to participate?
  (A) Contact the head office
  (B) Show up an hour early
  (C) Pay by check
  (D) Register with the reception desk

Unit 10
Travel

旅行

Vocabulary Building

 B-46 ▶ B-47

次の1～15はTOEIC頻出語句です。それぞれの意味を選択肢a～oから選び答えましょう。

1. accommodations （名）（　　）
2. belongings （名）（　　）
3. convenient （形）（　　）
4. destination （名）（　　）
5. effort （名）（　　）
6. expire （動）（　　）
7. issue （名）（　　）
8. occur （動）（　　）
9. reserve （動）（　　）
10. sightseeing （名）（　　）
11. temporary （形）（　　）
12. as a result （　　）
13. typical （形）（　　）
14. location （名）（　　）
15. view （名）（　　）

▶ 選択肢
a. その結果
b. 典型的な
c. 一時的な、臨時の
d. 眺め、見晴らし
e. 都合のよい、便利な
f. 宿泊施設
g. 起こる、発生する
h. 問題
i. 〜を予約する
j. 努力、取り組み
k. 期限が切れる
l. 所持品
m. 観光
n. 場所、所在地
o. 目的地

Listening Section

Tips for Part 3 and 4 | 部分を問う設問

Part 3と4における「部分を問う設問」とは、詳細な情報を尋ねる問題です。質問内容は多岐にわたります。質問が具体的なので、1単語を聞き逃しただけで正解できない可能性もあります。設問先読みによってキーワードを探しだし、ポイントを絞って聞き取ることが大切です。

設問例 What did the customer service send?

放送英文例 Have you received the document from our customer service department? ...

> 設問中のキーワードが、放送英文中でも聞こえてこないか集中する。聞こえてきたら、その前後に正答がある可能性が高い。

Training

質問Q1とQ2を先に読み、広告文の答え部分に下線を引きましょう(質問は読み返さない)。

Q1 When will the special offer end?　**Q2** What is available free of charge?

広告文　All of our designer frames are 15 percent off their usual prices! Remember, this special offer ends Friday, so hurry! And when you buy your new pair of glasses, you'll get a case for free. Come visit Clear Vision Center today!

Part 1　Photographs　写真描写問題　 B-48 ▶ B-49

4つの英文(A)〜(D)を聞き、写真を正しく描写するものを選んでマークしましょう。

1.

Ⓐ Ⓑ Ⓒ Ⓓ

Travel　旅行

2.

Ⓐ Ⓑ Ⓒ Ⓓ

Part 2 Question-Response 応答問題 🎧 B-50 ▶ B-54

問いかけに対する3つの応答(A)〜(C)を聞き、正しいものを選んでマークしましょう。

3. Ⓐ Ⓑ Ⓒ   4. Ⓐ Ⓑ Ⓒ   5. Ⓐ Ⓑ Ⓒ   6. Ⓐ Ⓑ Ⓒ   7. Ⓐ Ⓑ Ⓒ

Part 3 Short Conversations 会話問題 🎧 B-55 ▶ B-56

会話を聞き、3つの設問の答えとして適切なものを(A)〜(D)から選んでマークしましょう。

8. What are the speakers mainly discussing?
   (A) A personal trip
   (B) Park fees
   (C) Historical tours
   (D) Travel accommodations

   Ⓐ Ⓑ Ⓒ Ⓓ

9. What does the woman like best about Dudley Mountain?
   (A) Its hiking trails
   (B) Its inexpensive camping
   (C) Its scenery
   (D) Its holiday rates

   Ⓐ Ⓑ Ⓒ Ⓓ

10. What is suggested about the man's home?
    (A) It has long driveways.
    (B) It has clear views of Hope Lake.
    (C) It is hard to get to from work.
    (D) It is far from the countryside.

    Ⓐ Ⓑ Ⓒ Ⓓ

Part 4　Short Talks　説明文問題　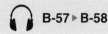

説明文を聞き、3つの設問の答えとして適切なものを(A)〜(D)から選んでマークしましょう。

11. What is the main purpose of the telephone message?

(A) To ask about preferences
(B) To ask about destinations
(C) To revise a departure date
(D) To schedule a meeting

Ⓐ Ⓑ Ⓒ Ⓓ

12. Why is the caller concerned?

(A) A deal has been canceled.
(B) Some offers may be temporary.
(C) Discounts are unavailable.
(D) First class is full.

Ⓐ Ⓑ Ⓒ Ⓓ

13. What is Ms. Horton asked to do?

(A) Call the office phone
(B) Reschedule her travel plans
(C) Send an e-mail
(D) Read a portable machine

Ⓐ Ⓑ Ⓒ Ⓓ

Reading Section

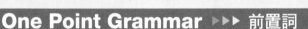

1. 基本の前置詞

〔1〕 **at**：特定の点を示します。時刻、場所、価格などとセットで使います。

例　at 9 A.M. / at the age of 20 / at the station / at a corner / at the lowest price / at extension 1015

〔2〕 **on**：何かに接しているのが基本のイメージです。

例　on the wall / on the train / on TV / on the phone / on Monday / on June 25

〔3〕 **in**：場所、空間、時間、状況、月を表す語とよくセットで使います。

例　in Tokyo / in the park / in the morning / in detail / in trouble / in May（※曜日だけなら on Monday、日付は on June 25）

〔4〕 **for**：対象、目的、方角などを表します。

例　① We apologize **for** our mistakes.
　　② AZ Sounds is known **for** the high quality of its audio appliances.

重要 until (till) と by の使い分け
① Let's wait for Tim here **until** five.　　[×] by
② I want to finish this work **by** five.　　[×] until

● 2.〈動詞＋前置詞〉

特定の動詞と一緒に用いる前置詞はセットで覚えましょう。

例 ① You can inform us **of** any change of address online.
　　② Most residents of this area rely **on** agriculture for their livelihoods.

● 3.〈形容詞＋前置詞〉

特定の形容詞と一緒に用いる前置詞はセットで覚えましょう。

例 ① You must punch your time card prior **to** beginning work.
　　② He is responsible **for** safety in this factory.

● 4. 予定や時に関する表現

ビジネスの話題でよく使う表現です。

例 ① The shipment arrived **on time**.
　　② The train is **behind schedule**.
　　③ All seminar participants must register **in advance**.

Tips for Part 5 and 6 ｜ 前置詞と接続詞の使い分け

前置詞（あるいは〈形容詞／副詞＋前置詞〉）と接続詞の使い分けが重要です。前置詞の後ろには名詞（相当の語句）、接続詞の後ろには文（節）が続きます。例えば、次の空所にはbecauseとbecause ofのどちらが入るか考えましょう。

（主語と動詞のある節になっている）

例 ① The game was canceled ------- it rained heavily.
　　② The game was canceled ------- the heavy rain.

（名詞相当語句になっている）

①は空所以降が節なのでbecause、②は名詞相当語句なのでbecause ofが入ります。また、よくあるミスに［×］I look forward to see you. がありますが、toは前置詞なのでI look forward to seeing you. と動名詞を続けます。

Training

選択肢から適切な表現を選んで、空欄に書き込みましょう。

1. Speaking _____ the CEO, Mr. Hong made a speech at the party.
2. I'm _____ planning Mr. White's retirement party.
3. I spent my vacation at home this year _____ traveling.
4. Mr. Clarkson would like to interview you _____ .
5. There is a one-hour train ride to the city _____ your two-hour flight.

選択肢 | in charge of / in addition to / in person / instead of / on behalf of

Part 5 Incomplete Sentences 短文穴埋め問題

英文の空所を埋めるのに適切な語句を、(A)〜(D)から選んでマークしましょう。

14. The family members will go to Canada ------- sightseeing this summer.
(A) to
(B) for
(C) on
(D) by

15. Mr. Rodriguez is looking forward to ------- some historical places in Madrid.
(A) visit
(B) visits
(C) visiting
(D) have visited

16. The student lived illegally in the U.K. ------- his visa expired.
(A) till
(B) by
(C) before
(D) after

17. Orangey Store changed its window display ------- an effort to attract more tourists.
(A) in
(B) on
(C) of
(D) at

18. ------- a tight budget, they had a memorable trip around Europe.
(A) Because
(B) Although
(C) Despite
(D) Conveniently

Part 6 Text Completion 長文穴埋め問題

英文の4つの空所を埋めるのに適切な語句を、(A)〜(D)から選んでマークしましょう。

Questions 19-22 refer to the following information.

Staisz Airlines
Luggage Policy

We make every effort to ensure that passengers' ------- are handled safely. We know that it is very annoying to lose luggage. -------.
　　　　　　　　　　　　　　　　　　　　　　19.　　　　　　　　　　　　　　　　　　　　　20.

Any lost luggage should be reported to our service center as soon as possible. You can be confident that we will ------- quickly. We can usually recover lost items ------- 24 hours.
　　　　　　　　　　　　　　　　　21.　　　　　　　　　　　　　　　　　　　　　　　　　22.

We will pay up to $200 to replace luggage and personal items once we verify these items are permanently lost or damaged.

19. (A) data
    (B) belongings
    (C) shipments
    (D) meals

20. (A) We can promise that these issues will not appear.
    (B) Our airline takes quick action when such incidents occur.
    (C) You will have to show your boarding pass at the gate.
    (D) We hope that you will have a pleasant flight.

21. (A) respond
    (B) demand
    (C) convert
    (D) allow

22. (A) by
    (B) until
    (C) around
    (D) within

Part 7 Reading Comprehension 読解問題

文書を読み、3つの設問の答えとして適切なものを(A) 〜 (D)から選んでマークしましょう。

Questions 23-25 refer to the following article.

Dream Vacation Magazine   April 26 Edition

Zunder Island: A Holiday Paradise
By Margo Wilder

Typical winter vacation spots have the problem of overcrowding. Zunder Island has few visitors even during its busiest months. As a result, vacationers can easily reserve spacious beachside cottages. The warm, distant island has many modern accommodations and forms of entertainment. In our next edition, the actress Martha Rye, our guest columnist, will review Demby Forest.

---

23. According to the article, what is a problem at typical winter vacation locations?

(A) They lack cottages.
(B) They are too distant.
(C) They have little entertainment.
(D) They are crowded.

24. What feature of Zunder Island is mentioned?

(A) It has many visitors during its busiest months.
(B) Vacationers are very friendly.
(C) Facilities are up-to-date.
(D) It is easily reachable by air.

25. Who is Martha Rye?

(A) A tourist
(B) A cottage owner
(C) A magazine publisher
(D) A performer

Unit 11
Finance

お金

Vocabulary Building

 B-59 ▶ B-60

次の1〜15はTOEIC頻出語句です。それぞれの意味を選択肢a〜oから選び答えましょう。

1. accounting (名) (　　)
2. bank account (　　)
3. benefit (動) (　　)
4. capital (名) (　　)
5. cashier (名) (　　)
6. due (形) (　　)
7. expense (名) (　　)
8. in charge of 〜 (　　)
9. inquiry (名) (　　)
10. invest (動) (　　)
11. property (名) (　　)
12. reduce (動) (　　)
13. reimbursement (名) (　　)
14. stock (名) (　　)
15. withdraw (動) (　　)

▶ 選択肢
a. 質問、問い合わせ b. 資本金 c. 投資する
d. 返済、払い戻し e. 〜を減らす f. 出費
g. レジ係 h. 利益を得る i. 不動産、財産
j. 株式、株（券） k. 〜を担当して l. 期限がきた、〜する予定になっている
m. （お金）を引き出す n. 銀行預金口座 o. 会計、経理（部）

Listening Section

Tips for Part 3 and 4 | 未来の行動を問う設問

「部分を問う設問」の一種ですが、Part 3と4の設問として特徴的なものに、「未来の行動を尋ねる設問」があります。この手の設問がある場合、放送される英文中では複数の行動が述べられるケースがほとんどです。それらの行動が、どのような順序で行われるのか、話の流れを正確に掴むことが決め手です。

> 「キャサリンと話す」と「キャビネットを調べる」。どちらが先かを把握する。

設問例 What will the man do next?

放送英文例 ... I'll go talk to Catherine, but first I'll check the cabinet. ...

Training

先に質問に目を通してから、英文を読み、答えになる部分に下線を引きましょう。

Q1 What will listeners hear next?

(英文) We'll listen to the guest speaker in a few minutes, but first, let's take a look at the history of the trade between our country and ancient China.

Q2 What does the man suggest the woman do?

(英文) Please take a seat over there. I'll call you when the documents are ready.

Part 1 Photographs 写真描写問題 B-61 ▶ B-62

4つの英文(A) 〜 (D)を聞き、写真を正しく描写するものを選んでマークしましょう。

1.

Ⓐ Ⓑ Ⓒ Ⓓ

Finance　お金

2.

Ⓐ Ⓑ Ⓒ Ⓓ

Part 2 Question-Response 応答問題   B-63 ▶ B-67

問いかけに対する3つの応答(A) 〜 (C)を聞き、正しいものを選んでマークしましょう。

3. Ⓐ Ⓑ Ⓒ   4. Ⓐ Ⓑ Ⓒ   5. Ⓐ Ⓑ Ⓒ   6. Ⓐ Ⓑ Ⓒ   7. Ⓐ Ⓑ Ⓒ

Part 3 Short Conversations 会話問題   B-68 ▶ B-69

会話を聞き、3つの設問の答えとして適切なものを(A) 〜 (D)から選んでマークしましょう。

8. Where does this conversation probably take place?
   (A) At a supermarket
   (B) In a park
   (C) At a bank
   (D) At City Hall

   Ⓐ Ⓑ Ⓒ Ⓓ

9. Why does the woman recommend the Growth Fund?
   (A) She thinks stocks will rise.
   (B) Only one dollar is needed.
   (C) Money can be taken out.
   (D) It pays good interest.

   Ⓐ Ⓑ Ⓒ Ⓓ

10. What is Savings Plus?
    (A) A capital city
    (B) A bank account
    (C) An interesting idea
    (D) An investment fund

    Ⓐ Ⓑ Ⓒ Ⓓ

Part 4　Short Talks　説明文問題　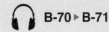

説明文を聞き、3つの設問の答えとして適切なものを(A)～(D)から選んでマークしましょう。

11. What is the speaker discussing?

(A) A project deadline
(B) A training program
(C) An investment goal
(D) A company policy

Ⓐ Ⓑ Ⓒ Ⓓ

12. What does the speaker mean when she says, "Nothing else"?

(A) A decision is final.
(B) A proposal is unchanged.
(C) Openings are unavailable.
(D) Payments are limited.

Ⓐ Ⓑ Ⓒ Ⓓ

13. Where most likely does Scott Taylor work?

(A) In IT
(B) In accounting
(C) In product design
(D) In quality control

Ⓐ Ⓑ Ⓒ Ⓓ

Reading Section

One Point Grammar ▶▶▶ 接続詞（接続副詞）

● **1. 話の流れを変える**

but, however, yet, although, though, even so, while など

 ① The company launched a big campaign, **but** its sales are still slow.
② **Although** she didn't have much experience, we decided to hire Ms. Santos.
※ in spite of, despite（前置詞）などとの使い分けに注意

● **2. 流れを変えずに話を続ける**

and, therefore など

例　They will meet at ten o'clock **and** discuss the problem.

● **3. 原因、理由を表す**

because, since, now that, as など

例　The meeting time was changed **because** Mr. Keen could not make it.
※ because of, due to などとの使い分けに注意。

● 4. 条件を表す

if, unless, as long as, in case など

例 ① **If** you have any questions, feel free to contact us.
② We cannot make much profit **unless** travel expenses are reduced.

● 5. 時を表す

when, while, before, by the time, until, since, as soon as など

例 ① We'll wait **until** she gets here.
② Please call me **as soon as** you get this message.

重要 セットで覚えておきたい表現

① either A or B: You can travel **either** by train **or** by ship.
② neither A nor B: **Neither** Martin **nor** Kate wanted to drive.
③ both A and B: The company has branch offices **both** in Japan **and** in Korea.
④ not only A but also B: She is relied on **not only** by her colleagues **but also** by her clients.

Tips for Part 5 and 6 | 意味のつながりを見極める

接続詞の問題では、空所前後の意味のつながりを見極めて、適切な接続詞を選択することがポイントです。次の例文には、becauseとalthoughどちらが入るか考えましょう。

> 空所前と後ろの関係性を見極める。

例 The football match was put off ------- it rained heavily.

空所以降が、空所以前の内容の理由になっているので、becauseを選びます。

Training

( ) 内の2語のうち、適切なほうを丸で囲みましょう。

1. We had to wait long (because / although) the flight was delayed.
2. The sun was shining, (yet / since) it was quite cold.
3. (Although / If) we missed the last deadline, our boss would never forgive us.
4. (While / During) younger workers lack confidence, older ones tend to overestimate their skills.
5. Ralph had enough experience, and (however / therefore) seemed the best candidate for the job.

Part 5　Incomplete Sentences　短文穴埋め問題

英文の空所を埋めるのに適切な語句を、(A) 〜 (D)から選んでマークしましょう。

14. The budget plan was due yesterday ------- the boss agreed to extend the deadline a little.

(A) but
(B) until
(C) if
(D) unless

15. Fares and hotel expenses will be paid ------- your forms are processed.

(A) but
(B) along
(C) once
(D) however

16. The prices were reduced mainly ------- increased foreign competition.

(A) though
(B) because
(C) due to
(D) while

17. Goldman Corporation's investment reports are written in ------- English and Spanish.

(A) both
(B) either
(C) every
(D) whether

18. Payment can be made either by cash ------- by automatic withdrawal from your bank account.

(A) and
(B) but
(C) or
(D) nor

Part 6 Text Completion 長文穴埋め問題

英文の4つの空所を埋めるのに適切な語句を、(A) 〜 (D)から選んでマークしましょう。

Questions 19-22 refer to the following letter.

Dear Ms. Yorba,

We are an organization committed to providing children everywhere with access to ------- . We operate free computer centers in low-income areas and send volunteer
19.
instructors to community centers. Yet, ------- like these are only possible with the help
20.
of kind people like you. Please donate whatever you can. ------- .
21.

You can not only place a check in the enclosed envelope ------- also donate through
22.
our Web site. We count on your generosity.

Sincerely,

Gerard Harrison
Public Relations Director

---

19. (A) education
(B) educationally
(C) educational
(D) educator

20. (A) people
(B) references
(C) wins
(D) activities

21. (A) You can expect high profits on your capital.
(B) Even small amounts are very much appreciated.
(C) Investors can get good tips at our seminars.
(D) Competition for the award is always intense.

22. (A) and
(B) but
(C) or
(D) neither

Part 7　Reading Comprehension　読解問題

文書を読み、3つの設問の答えとして適切なものを(A)〜(D)から選んでマークしましょう。

Questions 23-25 refer to the following document.

COMBINED UTILITIES INC.

Account information
Customer: Emma Simpson
Billing date: Feb. 5

Inquiries
Head office: 555-9934
Business hours: Mon.–Sat. (9:00 A.M.—5:00 P.M.)

Service period from Jan. 1 to Feb. 1

Current charges		
Water	15 units at $3.00 each	$ 45
Electricity	20 units at $3.50 each	$ 70
Total current charges		**$115**

Due by: Mar. 1 (a late charge will be applied as indicated on the back of the bill if the full amount is not paid by the due date)

Are you using energy efficiently? Call an adviser at 555-0246 for free advice on how to reduce your energy use.

---

23. What is the main purpose of this document?

(A) To pay fees
(B) To announce a penalty
(C) To offer advice
(D) To request payment

Ⓐ Ⓑ Ⓒ Ⓓ

24. When is the deadline?

(A) January 1
(B) February 1
(C) February 5
(D) March 1

Ⓐ Ⓑ Ⓒ Ⓓ

25. Which of the following is NOT mentioned?

(A) Business hours
(B) Gas fees
(C) A consultant
(D) Charge per unit

Ⓐ Ⓑ Ⓒ Ⓓ

Unit 12
Business

ビジネス

Vocabulary Building B-72 ▶ B-73

次の1〜15はTOEIC頻出語句です。それぞれの意味を選択肢a〜oから選び答えましょう。

1. ability (名) (　　)
2. as long as 〜 (　　)
3. bill (名) (　　)
4. carry out 〜 (　　)
5. demand (名) (　　)
6. full-time (形) (　　)
7. involve (動) (　　)
8. lawyer (名) (　　)
9. manufacturer (名) (　　)
10. previous (形) (　　)
11. reliable (形) (　　)
12. retire (動) (　　)
13. survey (名) (　　)
14. take over (　　)
15. text (動) (　　)

▶ 選択肢
- a. 〜を実施する
- b. 請求書、請求金額
- c. (仕事などを) 引き継ぐ
- d. 退職する、引退する
- e. 弁護士
- f. 〜である限り
- g. 以前の
- h. 信頼できる
- i. 〜できること、能力
- j. 調査
- k. 需要
- l. (携帯電話で)〜にメールを書いて送る
- m. 〜を含む
- n. 常勤の
- o. 製造業者、メーカー

Listening Section

Tips for Part 3 and 4 | 言い換え表現

Part 3 と 4 にかぎらず、TOEIC最大の特徴のひとつに、表現の「言い換え」があります。たとえば、会話でlowering costsと言っていたのを、選択肢ではreduce expensesと言い換えて、理解力を試してきます。この言い換えに対応するには、何と言っても語彙力です。TOEICの勉強を通じて語彙をどんどん増やせば、英語力も向上します。

Training

同じ内容を表現している語句同士を線で結びましょう。

1. due date   •   • a. supply
2. refrigerator   •   • b. quit one's job
3. provide   •   • c. deadline
4. resign   •   • d. appliance

Part 1 Photographs 写真描写問題   B-74 ▶ B-75

4つの英文(A)〜(D)を聞き、写真を正しく描写するものを選んでマークしましょう。

1.

Ⓐ Ⓑ Ⓒ Ⓓ

2.

Ⓐ Ⓑ Ⓒ Ⓓ

Part 2　Question-Response　応答問題　 B-76 ▸ B-79

問いかけに対する3つの応答(A)～(C)を聞き、正しいものを選んでマークしましょう。

3. Ⓐ Ⓑ Ⓒ　　**4.** Ⓐ Ⓑ Ⓒ　　**5.** Ⓐ Ⓑ Ⓒ　　**6.** Ⓐ Ⓑ Ⓒ

Part 3　Short Conversations　会話問題　 B-80 ▸ B-81

会話を聞き、3つの設問の答えとして適切なものを(A)～(D)から選んでマークしましょう。

KALEO DELIVERIES	
Services*	Package Arrival
Ultra	Same day
Prime	Overnight
Speedy	2-3 business days
Economy	4-6 business days

*Prices depend on the type of service chosen

7. What is the problem?
　(A) A package arrived late.
　(B) An energy bill is missing.
　(C) An expense is too high.
　(D) A monthly deadline was missed.
　　　　　　　　　　　　　Ⓐ Ⓑ Ⓒ Ⓓ

8. What did the man do yesterday?
　(A) Picked up a package
　(B) Canceled an option
　(C) Faxed some account details
　(D) Spoke with representatives
　　　　　　　　　　　　　Ⓐ Ⓑ Ⓒ Ⓓ

9. Look at the graphic. What service will the company switch to?
　(A) Ultra
　(B) Prime
　(C) Speedy
　(D) Economy
　　　　　　　　　　　　　Ⓐ Ⓑ Ⓒ Ⓓ

Part 4 Short Talks 説明文問題

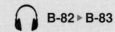

説明文を聞き、3つの設問の答えとして適切なものを(A)～(D)から選んでマークしましょう。

10. Who does the speaker introduce?

(A) A financial consultant
(B) A business professor
(C) An office executive
(D) A retirement planner

Ⓐ Ⓑ Ⓒ Ⓓ

11. According to the speaker, what will happen on July 27?

(A) A branch will open.
(B) An employee will leave the company.
(C) Interviews will take place.
(D) Promotions will be announced.

Ⓐ Ⓑ Ⓒ Ⓓ

12. What does Lisa Hong plan to do this quarter?

(A) Take more courses
(B) Become an assistant manager
(C) Promote a staff member
(D) Reduce expenses

Ⓐ Ⓑ Ⓒ Ⓓ

Reading Section

One Point Grammar ▶▶▶ 関係詞

先行詞	主格	所有格	目的格
人	who	whose	who/whom
モノ・動物	which	whose	which
両方	that	whose	that

先行詞	
場所を表す語	where
時を表す語	when
理由を表す語	why

※ what = the thing(s) which

例
① Crown Law Firm is seeking a new <u>lawyer</u> **who** has experience in patent filings.
② Tim works for a <u>manufacturer</u> **which/that** produces camping equipment.
③ This trade show is for <u>companies</u> **whose** speciality is the Asian market.
④ Please visit our <u>Web site</u> **where** you can check the special offer.
⑤ Do you remember **what** I asked you yesterday?

Tips for Part 5 and 6 | 関係詞を選ぶ手順

関係詞の問題では、まず先行詞を探し、「人」or「モノ（動物）」を確認。次に先行詞が空所以降の節でどのように働くかを考え、適切な関係詞を選びます。

> I used to work for the companyと考えられる。

例 Nelson Corp. is the company ------- I used to work for.

先行詞はモノであるthe company。これはI used to work forの目的語になっているので、目的格のwhichかthatを選択肢から選びます。

Training

(　　) 内の語句のうち、適切なものを丸で囲みましょう。

1. Customer satisfaction is the goal (who / which / what) we focus on.
2. The author (who / which / whose) books sell well was on TV last night.
3. Silicon Valley is (what / which / where) many top IT companies are headquartered.
4. (What / Those who) made the restaurant successful was its reasonable prices.

Part 5　Incomplete Sentences　短文穴埋め問題

英文の空所を埋めるのに適切な語句を、(A)〜(D)から選んでマークしましょう。

13. There was increased competition among manufactures ------- led to better products.
 (A) what
 (B) who
 (C) which
 (D) where

14. Employees in this section ------- wish to develop their skills should join this seminar.
 (A) who
 (B) whose
 (C) when
 (D) whenever

15. The new plant, ------- Mr. Sutton will supervise, is going to start operation next week.
 (A) that
 (B) which
 (C) where
 (D) those

16. David & Evelyn launched its new product in 1970, ------- it became well-known later.
 (A) when
 (B) where
 (C) for which
 (D) rather than

Part 6 Text Completion 長文穴埋め問題

英文の4つの空所を埋めるのに適切な語句を、(A)〜(D)から選んでマークしましょう。

Questions 17-20 refer to the following letter.

Dear Mr. Zhukov,

We hope your firm will rent space at our trade show in December. This is an ------- way to display your goods and services.
                                                                              17.

It is also a great way of meeting potential customers ------- come from all over the
                                                        18.
world. Suppliers, researchers, and the media will also be present. ------- .
                                                                     19.

Thanks to that, there is high demand for the prime sections. Therefore, it is a good idea to reserve your ------- as soon as you can. To get started on this, please contact
                        20.
me.

Yours sincerely,

Veronica Fields
E-mail: v.fields@globalmachshow.net
Sales and Marketing, Global Machinery Show

---

17. (A) ideal
(B) ideally
(C) idealize
(D) idealistic

ⓐⒷⒸⒹ

18. (A) who
(B) whose
(C) whom
(D) which

ⓐⒷⒸⒹ

19. (A) Your ID cards should arrive in just 3-5 days.
(B) Rules prohibit us from discussing some information.
(C) Arrive by 10:00 A.M. to make your purchase.
(D) Your company will receive global attention.

ⓐⒷⒸⒹ

20. (A) building
(B) spot
(C) products
(D) conference

ⓐⒷⒸⒹ

Part 7 Reading Comprehension 読解問題

文書を読み、3つの設問の答えとして適切なものを(A)〜(D)から選んでマークしましょう。

Questions 21-25 refer to the following advertisement, e-mail, and résumé.

JOB VACANCY

Jones & Johnston Law Firm is now accepting applications for the position of a full-time researcher in Los Angeles. This opening involves legal research, editing, and general office duties. Legal experience and an ability to work most weekends are a must. Applicants should have computer skills and excellent written English. We provide three months' initial training in our San Diego office.

Please submit your résumé and a letter of application by e-mail to Mr. Eric Gonzales at ericg@jandjlaw.com by August 15. Interviews will begin from September 1 and the position will start on September 15.

E-mail

From:	Patricia Dolan <pdolan33@trymail.com>
To:	Eric Gonzales <ericg@jandjlaw.com>
Date:	August 5
Subject:	Job application
Attachment:	📎 résumé

Dear Mr. Gonzales,

I am writing to apply for the position of researcher, as advertised in this month's issue of *Inside Law*.

This job interests me greatly because it matches my experience perfectly. I have worked as a legal secretary in the past and, although I am out of work at the moment, I keep myself up-to-date with legal issues.

My previous job involved a lot of work on computers, including creating spreadsheets and writing legal documents.

Please find attached a copy of my résumé.

I am available for an interview immediately and look forward to hearing from you.

Yours sincerely,
Patricia Dolan

PATRICIA DOLAN

208a Melburn Drive, San Diego, CA
pdolan33@trymail.com

Date of birth:	11/25/1984
Key skills:	Word processing; Legal experience; Reliable and hard-working
Work experience:	2012–2015 Gryler Legal Services, Legal secretary
Duties: Creating legal reports and spreadsheets; Assisting with research.
	2010–2012 Fortnam Fashions, Assistant to CEO
Duties: Scheduling; Typing; Answering telephone
Interests:	I volunteer every Sunday at a pet rescue center. I also enjoy mountain biking and playing basketball.

21. What kind of job is being advertised?
  (A) Lawyer
  (B) Researcher
  (C) Secretary
  (D) Editor

22. When is the deadline for applications?
  (A) August 5
  (B) August 15
  (C) September 1
  (D) September 15

23. Why is Ms. Dolan interested in the position?
  (A) She has done similar work before.
  (B) She likes writing.
  (C) She knows the firm well.
  (D) She lives near the company.

24. What will Ms. Dolan most likely do if she is hired?
  (A) Write articles for *Inside Law*
  (B) Move to San Francisco
  (C) Attend training near her home
  (D) Quit her current job

25. Which requirement for the job does Ms. Dolan NOT meet?
  (A) Legal experience
  (B) Computer skills
  (C) Excellent written English
  (D) Ability to work weekends

Tips for Part 7 | 文中の単語を言い換える問題

Part 7で特徴的な設問に、パッセージ中の1語を取りだして、その意味を問うものがあります。これもp. 111で説明した「言い換え表現」の一種。語彙力強化が最大の対策です。

例 In the e-mail, the word "run" in paragraph 2, line 3, is closest in meaning to
  (A) manage / (B) make / (C) decide / (D) escape

Post-test (問題音声は教師用音源に収録)

LISTENING TEST T-26 ▶ T-28

In the Listening test, you will be asked to demonstrate how well you understand spoken English. The entire Listening test will last approximately 13 minutes. There are four parts, and directions are given for each part. You must mark your answers on the separate answer sheet. Do not write your answers in your test book.

PART 1

Directions: For each question in this part, you will hear four statements about a picture in your test book. When you hear the statements, you must select the one statement that best describes what you see in the picture. Then find the number of the question on your answer sheet and mark your answer. The statements will not be printed in your test book and will be spoken only one time.

Statement (C), "They're sitting at a table," is the best description of the picture, so you should select answer (C) and mark it on your answer sheet.

1.

1.

PART 2

 T-29 ▶ T-37

Directions: You will hear a question or statement and three responses spoken in English. They will not be printed in your test book and will be spoken only one time. Select the best response to the question or statement and mark the letter (A), (B), or (C) on your answer sheet.

3. Ⓐ Ⓑ Ⓒ
4. Ⓐ Ⓑ Ⓒ
5. Ⓐ Ⓑ Ⓒ
6. Ⓐ Ⓑ Ⓒ
7. Ⓐ Ⓑ Ⓒ
8. Ⓐ Ⓑ Ⓒ
9. Ⓐ Ⓑ Ⓒ
10. Ⓐ Ⓑ Ⓒ

PART 3

T-38 ▶ T-44

Directions: You will hear some conversations between two or more people. You will be asked to answer three questions about what the speakers say in each conversation. Select the best response to each question and mark the letter (A), (B), (C), or (D) on your answer sheet. The conversations will not be printed in your test book and will be spoken only one time.

GO ON TO THE NEXT PAGE

11. Why is the woman calling?
    (A) To confirm a price
    (B) To request a service
    (C) To offer feedback
    (D) To ask about a schedule
    Ⓐ Ⓑ Ⓒ Ⓓ

12. What does the man ask the woman about?
    (A) Her departure date
    (B) Her destination
    (C) Her accommodations
    (D) Her flight number
    Ⓐ Ⓑ Ⓒ Ⓓ

13. Where will the woman stay in Mexico City?
    (A) In a hotel
    (B) In company housing
    (C) With a coworker
    (D) With a family member
    Ⓐ Ⓑ Ⓒ Ⓓ

14. What are the speakers mainly discussing?
    (A) Sales plans
    (B) Open positions
    (C) Accounting regulations
    (D) Employee income
    Ⓐ Ⓑ Ⓒ Ⓓ

15. What is the woman unable to find?
    (A) Business records
    (B) News releases
    (C) Staff bonuses
    (D) Meeting schedules
    Ⓐ Ⓑ Ⓒ Ⓓ

16. What does the man recommend doing?
    (A) Contacting the board of directors
    (B) Waiting for a decision
    (C) Making an announcement
    (D) Submitting financial statements
    Ⓐ Ⓑ Ⓒ Ⓓ

17. What does the woman say about Simona Marks?
    (A) She is a great new employee.
    (B) She is skilled at giving talks.
    (C) She is working on new devices.
    (D) She is recruiting company staff.
    Ⓐ Ⓑ Ⓒ Ⓓ

18. What do the men suggest about the laptops?
    (A) They can be picked up from IT.
    (B) They can be issued in three days.
    (C) They are ready for distribution.
    (D) They are upgraded from last quarter.
    Ⓐ Ⓑ Ⓒ Ⓓ

19. Why does the woman say, "We're depending on that"?
    (A) A job may be too difficult.
    (B) An action is important.
    (C) A project should be promoted.
    (D) A request has to be reviewed.
    Ⓐ Ⓑ Ⓒ Ⓓ

PART 4   T-45 ▶ T-49

Directions: You will hear some talks given by a single speaker. You will be asked to answer three questions about what the speaker says in each talk. Select the best response to each question and mark the letter (A), (B), (C), or (D) on your answer sheet. The talks will not be printed in your test book and will be spoken only one time.

20. Who most likely are the listeners?
    (A) Customers
    (B) Stockholders
    (C) Sales staff
    (D) Suppliers

21. Why does the speaker congratulate the listeners?
    (A) They arrived on short notice.
    (B) They achieved a goal.
    (C) They designed a Web site.
    (D) They provided helpful feedback.

22. What is scheduled to happen on January 6?
    (A) People will get together.
    (B) A new department will be launched.
    (C) Store sales will be started.
    (D) Survey details will be issued.

International Convention Center

Floor 4:	Cafeteria
Floor 3:	Private Rooms
Floor 2:	Press Conferences
Floor 1:	Exhibitions

23. Where most likely are the listeners?
    (A) At an awards ceremony
    (B) At a job fair
    (C) At a shareholder conference
    (D) At a trade show

24. Look at the graphic. Where can people see Thomas Lee speak?
    (A) On Floor 1
    (B) On Floor 2
    (C) On Floor 3
    (D) On Floor 4

25. What are listeners requested to do?
    (A) Wear identification
    (B) Avoid taking photos
    (C) Remain on the grounds
    (D) Write about a seminar

This is the end of the listening test. Turn to Part 5 in your test book.

READING TEST

In the Reading test, you will read a variety of texts and answer several different types of reading comprehension questions. The entire Reading test will last 20 minutes. There are three parts, and directions are given for each part. You are encouraged to answer as many questions as possible within the time allowed.

You must mark your answers on the separate answer sheet. Do not write your answers in your test book.

PART 5

Directions: A word or phrase is missing in each of the sentences below. Four answer choices are given below each sentence. Select the best answer to complete the sentence. Then mark the letter (A), (B), (C), or (D) on your answer sheet.

26. Ms. Tang will be honored at tonight's meeting because of her contribution to ------- company.
    (A) us
    (B) we
    (C) our
    (D) ours

27. The advertising department will ------- a survey on consumers' attitudes toward their new product.
    (A) record
    (B) involve
    (C) practice
    (D) conduct

28. ------- the inclement weather, Mr. Ryan's flight arrived at San Fernando International Airport on time.
    (A) In spite of
    (B) As if
    (C) Although
    (D) Instead of

29. ------- to the special seminar on communication have been sent to all the employees.
    (A) Invite
    (B) Invitations
    (C) Inviting
    (D) Invitation

30. This information is based on the annual report ------- by the London School of Economics.
    (A) published
    (B) was published
    (C) publish
    (D) publishing

31. Most employees who completed the evaluation rated their working conditions as ------- good or excellent.
    (A) both
    (B) between
    (C) either
    (D) neither

32. The public relations department requires the ------- statistics on the use of online shopping.

(A) late
(B) later
(C) lately
(D) latest

33. The construction work of the shopping mall in Inchon ------- by the end of the next month.

(A) completes
(B) was completed
(C) has been completing
(D) will be completed

34. We are proud to be able to keep our rates ------- and provide prompt service in this financially difficult time.

(A) competes
(B) competition
(C) competitive
(D) competitively

35. Sun Travels does not allow its employees ------- overtime more than 20 hours per week.

(A) work
(B) working
(C) to work
(D) have worked

36. ------- you learned during this course will help you handle various difficulties you may face in society.

(A) What
(B) When
(C) Which
(D) If

GO ON TO THE NEXT PAGE

PART 6

Directions: Read the texts that follow. A word, phrase, or sentence is missing in parts of each text. Four answer choices for each question are given below the text. Select the best answer to complete the text. Then mark the letter (A), (B), (C), or (D) on your answer sheet.

Questions 37-40 refer to the following announcement.

Posted at: 10:23 A.M.

Natalia Kowalski has been named Employee of the Year. Natalia works ------- a clerk in our mailroom.
37.

-------. Yet, she has proposed many useful tips on how we can improve our
38.
processes there. -------, she has created a plan for faster mail sorting. Her supervisor,
39.
Katy Duvall, told human resources that "Natalia is always doing the kinds of things

------- add value to the firm." As the winner, she will receive €100 and one paid day off
40.
from work.

37. (A) of
    (B) as
    (C) on
    (D) through

38. (A) Some might see her job as routine.
    (B) Others hope she will delay her retirement.
    (C) She approved the new policies right away.
    (D) Many people helped with her responsibilities.

39. (A) Almost
    (B) Nevertheless
    (C) Specifically
    (D) Likewise

40. (A) whom
    (B) whose
    (C) who
    (D) that

PART 7

Directions: In this part you will read a selection of texts, such as magazine and newspaper articles, e-mails, and instant messages. Each text or set of texts is followed by several questions. Select the best answer for each question and mark the letter (A), (B), (C), or (D) on your answer sheet.

Questions 41-42 refer to the following document.

Minelli Corporation
www.minellicorp.co.au.

Estimate Date:
January 13

Installation Estimate for:
Ms. Angelina Martinez
22 Crawford Avenue

Identification Number:
285X93

Product(s):	• 5 Window alarms • 3 Door alarms • Keypad entry system

Product cost	A$832.19
Labor cost	A$157.43
Total cost	A$989.62

If you wish to go forward with this project, please e-mail us at: orders@minellicorp.co.au. Please reference the estimate number above in the subject line.

41. What type of business most likely is Minelli Corporation?
   (A) A real estate developer
   (B) A landscaping business
   (C) An IT firm
   (D) A security company

42. What information is NOT mentioned in the estimate?
   (A) Identification number
   (B) Product expense
   (C) Completion date
   (D) Work costs

GO ON TO THE NEXT PAGE

Questions 43-45 refer to the following letter.

Mr. Carlos Hernandez
128 Moorehouse Avenue
Huntsford
HT7 3RS

Dear Mr. Hernandez,

Thank you for your letter of September 30 regarding the road construction on Moorehouse Avenue.

—[1]—. We are sorry that the noise is affecting your sleep, but work must be conducted in the early morning to avoid causing rush-hour traffic. —[2]—. We sent information to all residents two months before work started. We hope you will understand the need for this construction now. —[3]—. The project will widen Moorehouse Avenue, making your neighborhood safer and more convenient for all residents.

—[4]—. Work will finish two weeks ahead of schedule.

Thank you for your patience.

Sincerely,

Erica Jones
Erica Jones
Planning Department
Huntsford City Council

43. What did Mr. Hernandez most likely write on September 30?
    (A) A request for information
    (B) A complaint about noise
    (C) A thank-you note
    (D) A suggestion for road construction

44. Why is there construction on Moorehouse Avenue?
    (A) To make repairs
    (B) To build a new road
    (C) To install security cameras
    (D) To make the road bigger

45. In which of the positions marked [1], [2], [3], and [4] does the following sentence best belong?

    "We also received some positive news from the site."

    (A) [1]
    (B) [2]
    (C) [3]
    (D) [4]

Questions 46-50 refer to the following product information, online review, and response.

The Ventor Mark II—A new generation of air conditioner

In the heat of high summer, the Ventor Mark II will keep your work or living space at a cool, comfortable temperature.

Features

- Air can be either focused on one part of the room for personal activities or spread over a wide area for groups.
- Silent operation
- Slim body and clean, white finish
- Easy-clean filters and clean filter alarm

---

https://www.ventor-products.com/ventor2/reviews

July 7

I recently purchased this model for my home. I decided on the Ventor mainly because I have the Mark I in my office, and it has worked perfectly for a number of years. Sadly, I cannot say the same for this model.

The product description advertises silent operation. Well, that is certainly not the case with mine! I couldn't sleep at night due to the noise. The clean filter alarm sounds every twelve hours, which is very annoying! Also, the white finish looks cheap. I enjoy the other features but, despite this, I cannot recommend this product to anyone.

Saeed Latif

---

https://www.ventor-products.com/ventor2/reviews

July 10

Dear Mr. Latif,

Firstly, I would like to apologize for the poor experience you have had with the Ventor Mark II.

From reading your comment, it seems like the model you bought has a mechanical problem. The Mark II should operate silently so there may be some loose parts causing the noise. As for the filter alarm, this is a recognized error in production and we are working on a software update.

We would like to offer you both a replacement product and a $100 gift card for your inconvenience. Please get in touch with us directly at the e-mail address below and we will make arrangements immediately.

Sincerely,

Joan Watkins
Customer relations
jwatkins@ventor-products.com

46. Which feature of the Ventor Mark II does Mr. Latif most likely like?
   (A) The focused air feature
   (B) The color
   (C) The silent operation
   (D) The filter alarm

47. In the online review, the word "case" in paragraph 2, line 1 is closest in meaning to
   (A) bag
   (B) reason
   (C) situation
   (D) chance

48. What is indicated about Mr. Latif?
   (A) He works from home.
   (B) He has had another of the company's products.
   (C) He recommends the product.
   (D) He can sleep well due to the product.

49. According to the response, why is Mr. Latif's air conditioner noisy?
   (A) Some parts are moving.
   (B) He broke the product.
   (C) It does not have a silent feature.
   (D) It requires a software update.

50. What does Ms. Watkins offer Mr. Latif?
   (A) A full refund
   (B) A visit by a mechanic
   (C) Another air conditioner
   (D) One hundred dollars in cash

STOP! This is the end of the test. If you finish before time is called, you may go back to Parts 5, 6, and 7 and check your work.

頻出語句リスト

本書で出題された446語句を意味付きで整理します。語彙力のチェックにご利用ください。参照先は出題ユニットのパートを示しています。

（例：「U7-P7」= Unit 7 の Part 7 で出題）

A

- a little bit 少しだけ U1-P4
- ability 名 〜できること、能力 U12-P7
- acceptance 名 受諾、賛成 U8-P7
- accessible 形 行くことができる U2-P5
- accommodations 名 宿泊施設 U10-P3
- according to 〜 〜によれば U4-P2
- account 名 口座 U4-P4
- accounting 名 会計、経理 U11-P2
- achievement 名 成果、功績 U8-P7
- ad campaign 広告キャンペーン U2-P5
- address 動 〜に演説する U9-P4
  動 〜に取り組む U9-P5
- admission 名 入場（料） U2-P6
- advance 形 事前の U2-P6
- advertise 動 〜を宣伝する U2-P7
- affect 動 〜に影響する U3-P6
- afford 動 〜を買う余裕がある U1-P2
- agenda 名 議題 U9-P3
- agree 動 同意する U4-P6
- aircraft 名 航空機 U3-P4
- aisle 名 通路 U1-P6
- amount 名 金額、量 U11-P6
- annoying 形 いらだたせる U10-P6
- annual 形 年1回の、毎年の U2-P6
- anticipate 動 〜を予期する U8-P7
- appear 動 〜のように見える、思われる U7-P6
- appliance 名 電化製品、器具 U1-P5
- applicant 名 応募者 U12-P7
- application 名 応募 U4-P6
- apply 動 申し込む U2-P7
  動 〜を適用する U3-P6
- appointment 名 （病院などの）予約、（会う）約束 U2-P3
- appreciate 動 〜に感謝する U7-P3
- artwork 名 芸術作品 U7-P6
- as a result その結果 U10-P7
- as long as 〜 〜である限り U12-P3
- as soon as possible できるだけ早く U6-P3
- as usual いつも通り U12-P2
- assemble 動 〜を組み立てる U1-P3
- attach 動 〜を添付する U4-P7
- attend 動 〜に出席する U9-P2
- attract 動 〜をひきつける U10-P5
- attraction 名 アトラクション、呼び物 U7-P6
- author 名 作者、著者 U7-P2
- available 形 利用可能な、入手可能な U3-P4
- avoid 動 〜を避ける U1-P6

B

- bank account 銀行預金口座 U11-P3
- banquet 名 晩餐会 U6-P5
- battery 名 電池 U2-P2
- be about to do まさに〜しようとしている U3-P7
- be committed to 〜 （全力で）〜に取り組む U11-P6
- be supposed to do 〜することになっている U6-P3
- be up to X X次第である U8-P6
- be worth X Xの価値がある U5-P7
- belongings 名 所持品 U10-P2
- benefit 動 利益を得る U1-P6
- bidder 名 入札者 U7-P6
- bill 動 〜に請求書を送る U11-P7
  名 請求書、請求金額 U12-P3
- blueprint 名 青写真、設計図 U9-P2
- board 動 （飛行機・バスなど）に乗り込む U3-P4
  名 取締役会 U8-P2
- book 動 〜を予約する U7-P2
- branch 名 支店、支社 U4-P3
- brochure 名 パンフレット U2-P3
- budget 名 予算 U1-P7
- business 名 商売、営業 U7-P6

C

- cabinet 名 整理戸棚 U2-P1
- calm 形 冷静な、落ち着いた U2-P7
- candidate 名 志望者、候補者 U4-P5
- capital 名 資本金 U11-P3
- carry out 〜 〜を実施する U12-P2
- cashier 名 レジ係 U11-P1
- casually 副 カジュアルに、気軽に U2-P2
- catch 動 （乗り物）に乗る U3-P3
- caterer 名 仕出し業者 U5-P6
- Celsius 名 摂氏 U2-P4
- certainly 副 確かに、ほんとうに U8-P7
- chair 動 〜の議長を務める U9-P2
- charge 動 （料金）を請求する U1-P3
  名 料金、請求金額 U11-P7
- choice 名 選択 U1-P4
- client 名 顧客 U3-P3
- closing remark 閉会の辞 U9-P7
- closure 名 （一時的な）閉鎖 U3-P6
- comment 動 意見を述べる U6-P2

☐	commuter	名 通勤［通学］者	U3-P5	☐	dish	名 料理 U5-P1
☐	compare	動 ～を比べる	U9-P5	☐	distant	形 遠い U10-P7
☐	competition	名 競争	U12-P5	☐	distribute	動 ～をばらまく U7-P5
☐	competitive	形 競争力のある	U9-P4	☐	donate	動 ～を寄付する U11-P6
☐	complaint	名 不満、苦情	U5-P7	☐	drawer	名 引き出し U2-P1
☐	complex	形 複雑な	U5-P6	☐	dress	動 服を着る U2-P2
☐	concern	名 心配（事）	U3-P4	☐	due	形 ～する予定になっている、期限がきた U11-P5
☐	conference	名 会議、協議会	U9-P2	☐	due to ～	～が原因で U3-P4
☐	confident	形 確信している、自信がある U10-P6		☐	duty	名 職務、義務 U4-P7

E

☐ confirm	動 ～を確認する	U2-P3	
☐ connect	動 接続する	U6-P2	
☐ consider X Y	動 XをYと考える	U3-P5	
☐ contact	動 ～に連絡する	U6-P3	
☐ contact information	連絡先	U6-P7	
☐ contain	動 ～を含む	U12-P2	
☐ convenient	形 都合のよい、便利な	U10-P2	
☐ convince	動 ～を納得させる	U3-P3	
☐ cooperation	名 協力	U8-P6	
☐ corporation	名 企業	U1-P5	
☐ count on	～をあてにする	U11-P6	
☐ count X in	Xを数に入れる	U7-P2	
☐ coupon	名 クーポン、割引券	U5-P4	
☐ cover	動 （費用など）をまかなう、負担する	U11-P4	
☐ coworker	名 同僚	U4-P3	
☐ cross	動 ～を横断する	U3-P1	
☐ current	形 現在の、最新の	U11-P7	
☐ currently	副 現在は	U6-P4	
☐ customer	名 顧客、取引先	U1-P5	

☐ education　名 教育　U4-P3
☐ efficiently　副 効率的に　U11-P7
☐ effort　名 努力、取り組み　U10-P5
☐ electricity　名 電気　U2-P2
☐ electronics　名 電子機器　U1-P2
☐ employment　名 雇用　U4-P7
☐ enclosed　形 同封の　U7-P7
☐ engineer　名 技術者　U4-P3
☐ ensure　動 ～を保証する、確実にする　U9-P4
☐ enter　動 ～に入る　U3-P1
☐ entrance　名 入口　U5-P3
　　　　　　名 入場　U7-P6
☐ envelope　名 封筒　U11-P6
☐ examine　動 ～を調べる、検討する　U6-P1
☐ executive　名 （企業などの）役員、幹部　U12-P4
☐ exhibit　名 展示（会）　U7-P4
☐ exhibition　名 展示　U7-P5
☐ expect　動 ～を期待する、予期する　U7-P3
☐ expense　名 出費　U11-P5
☐ expert　名 専門家　U7-P6
☐ expertise　名 専門知識　U4-P7
☐ expiration　名 （期限の）満了　U1-P6
☐ expire　動 期限が切れる　U10-P5
☐ extend　動 ～を延長する、拡大する　U11-P5
☐ extension　名 （電話の）内線　U6-P4

D

☐ deadline　名 締切　U11-P4
☐ deal　名 取引、契約　U10-P4
☐ decision　名 決定、決意　U8-P7
☐ decline　動 衰える、減少する　U9-P4
☐ decorate　動 ～を飾る　U7-P1
☐ degree　名 度（温度の単位）　U2-P4
☐ delay　名 遅延　U3-P7
　　　動 ～を延期する　U3-P7
☐ delightful　形 とても楽しい　U5-P7
☐ deliver　動 ～を届ける、配達する　U1-P3
☐ delivery　名 配達　U1-P2
☐ demand　名 需要　U12-P6
☐ depart　動 出発する　U3-P2
☐ department　形 部署、課　U4-P3
☐ describe　動 ～を描写する、説明する　U6-P5
☐ designated　形 指定の　U3-P5
☐ desired　形 望ましい　U2-P5
☐ destination　名 目的地　U10-P4
☐ detail　名 詳細　U12-P3
☐ diner　名 食事をする人　U5-P1
☐ discuss　動 ～について話し合う、議論する　U4-P6

F

☐ face　動 ～に面する　U7-P1
☐ facility　名 施設、設備　U6-P3
☐ farm　名 農場　U5-P7
☐ feature　動 ～を特集する、～を（大きく）扱う　U7-P7
　　　　　名 特徴　U10-P7
☐ fee　名 料金、手数料　U11-P7
☐ file　動 （書類）をファイルにとじる　U9-P1
☐ fill out ～　～に記入する　U7-P2
☐ find out ～　～を見つけ出す　U2-P7
☐ firm　名 会社　U12-P6
☐ fit　動 ぴったり収まる　U3-P3
☐ fix　動 ～を修理する　U9-P1

131

☐ flier	名 ちらし	U7-P5
☐ form	名 書式、用紙	U8-P3
☐ frightened	形 おびえた	U3-P2
☐ fulfill	動 ～を果たす、実現する	U8-P7
☐ full-time	形 常勤の	U12-P7
☐ fund	名 資金	U11-P3

G

☐ garage	名 車庫、ガレージ	U3-P1
☐ generosity	名 気前のよさ、寛大さ	U11-P6
☐ get	動 着く、到着する	U3-P7
☐ get on	（乗り物）に乗る	U3-P1
☐ give away ～	～を無料で与える	U5-P4
☐ graduate	名 卒業生	U12-P4
☐ greet	動 ～を出迎える	U5-P3
☐ guarantee	動 ～を保証する	U9-P6

H

☐ hallway	名 廊下	U3-P1
☐ hand X to Y	動 XをYに手渡す	U3-P2
☐ handle	動 ～を扱う	U10-P6
☐ hang	動 ～を掛ける	U2-P1
☐ hang up	電話を切る	U6-P4
☐ head	名（組織の）長、リーダー	U4-P3
☐ head office	本社、本店	U9-P7
☐ headquartered	形 本社がある	U4-P7
☐ hesitate	動 ためらう	U7-P5
☐ honestly	副 正直に	U1-P7
☐ host	動 ～を主催する	U2-P6
☐ human resources	人事部（課）、人材	U4-P3

I

☐ I'm afraid ～	（好ましくないことについて）～と思う	U2-P3
☐ ideal	形 理想的な	U10-P3
☐ illegally	副 違法に	U10-P5
☐ immediately	副 すぐに	U6-P2
☐ impressive	形 印象的な、感動的な	U5-P7
☐ improvement	名 改善、上達	U6-P6
☐ in advance	前もって	U8-P4
☐ in charge of ～	～を担当して	U11-P4
☐ in detail	詳細に	U6-P2
☐ in line	一列になって	U3-P5
☐ incident	名 事件、出来事	U10-P6
☐ include	動 ～を含む	U7-P5
☐ income	名 収入、所得	U11-P3
☐ indicate	動 ～を示す	U7-P4
☐ industry	名 業界	U9-P6
☐ inform X of ～	Xに～を知らせる	U1-P6
☐ inquiry	名 質問、問い合わせ	U11-P7
☐ install	動 ～を設置する、導入する	U6-P6
☐ instead	副 その代わりに	U9-P6
☐ instead of ～	～の代わりに	U3-P4

☐ institution	名 組織、団体	U7-P5
☐ instruction	名 取扱説明書、指示	U1-P3
☐ instrument	名 器具、楽器	U7-P7
☐ insurance	名 保険	U2-P3
☐ intense	形 激しい、強烈な	U11-P6
☐ interest	名 利息、金利	U11-P3
☐ interview	名 面接	U4-P4
☐ invest	動 投資する	U11-P3
☐ investment	名 投資	U11-P3
☐ investor	名 投資家	U4-P7
☐ invite	動 ～に勧める	U7-P4
☐ involve	動 ～を含む	U12-P7
☐ issue	名 問題	U10-P6
☐ item	名 商品	U1-P2

J

☐ journal	名 定期刊行物、雑誌	U7-P5

K

☐ knowledge	名 知識	U4-P7

L

☐ laboratory	名 研究所	U8-P5
☐ ladder	名 はしご	U12-P1
☐ lane	名 車線	U3-P6
☐ last	動 継続する	U9-P4
☐ launch	動 ～を売り出す、開始する	U7-P6
☐ law firm	法律事務所	U12-P7
☐ lawyer	名 弁護士	U12-P7
☐ lean	動 ～を寄りかからせる	U12-P1
☐ light	名 信号（機）	U3-P1
☐ locate	動 ～を位置づける	U4-P5
☐ location	名 場所、所在地	U10-P7
☐ logical	形 論理的な	U5-P6
☐ look for ～	～を探す	U1-P7
☐ luggage	名 荷物	U10-P6

M

☐ machinery	名 機械	U9-P6
☐ mainly	副 主に、主として	U11-P5
☐ maintain	動 ～を維持する、保つ	U8-P6
☐ make it	うまくやり遂げる、間に合う	U5-P2
☐ manufacturer	名 製造業者、メーカー	U12-P5
☐ market	動 ～を売り出す	U4-P4
☐ marketing	名 マーケティング	U11-P2
☐ match	動 ～に調和する、合う	U7-P2
☐ meal	名 食事	U5-P4
☐ mention	動 ～に言及する	U4-P7
☐ merchandise	名 商品	U6-P1
☐ mind	動 ～を気にする、いやがる	U7-P2

N

nervous	形 緊張した、神経質な	U2-P7

O

occur	動 起こる、発生する	U10-P6
offer	動 ～を申し出る、提供する	U2-P7
	名 申し出、割引	U5-P4
office supplies	事務用品、筆記用具	U8-P1
on behalf of ～	～に代わって、代表して	U6-P3
on display	陳列して、展示して	U1-P1
on duty	勤務時間中で	U8-P2
on sale	売りに出されて、特価で	U1-P2
on time	時間通りに	U3-P4
ongoing	形 進行中の	U4-P6
(by) oneself	独力で、ひとりで	U1-P3
opening	名 欠員、就職口	U4-P7
operate	動 ～を経営する、運営する	U11-P6
order	動 ～を注文する	U1-P3
organization	名 組織、団体	U11-P6
otherwise	副 さもないと	U6-P4
outlet	名 コンセント	U9-P6
outstanding	形 傑出した	U5-P6
overcrowding	名 超過密の状態	U10-P7

P

pack	動 ～を梱包する	U3-P3
package	名 小包	U12-P3
park	動 ～を駐車する	U3-P5
parking lot	駐車場	U7-P3
participant	名 参加者	U2-P7
participation	名 参加	U2-P6
passenger	名 乗客	U3-P1
patient	名 患者	U2-P3
payment	名 支払い	U2-P3
performance	名 公演、演奏	U7-P5
	名 業績、成績	U8-P7
personnel	名 人事部、社員	U4-P7
photocopier	名 コピー機	U8-P3
pillow	名 枕	U2-P1
place	動 ～を置く	U2-P1
place an order	注文をする	U1-P5
pleasant	形 気持ちのよい	U10-P6
policy	名 方針	U11-P4
position	名 職、仕事	U4-P5
potential	形 見込みのある	U2-P7
predict	動 ～を予測する	U2-P4
prefer	動 ～の方を好む	U5-P2
preference	名 好み	U10-P4
president	名 社長	U8-P2
previous	形 以前の	U12-P7
price tag	値札	U1-P7
procedure	名 手順、やり方	U6-P5
process	動 ～を処理する	U11-P5
production	名 生産	U9-P6

profit	名 利益	U9-P4
profitable	形 利益になる	U11-P2
prohibit X from doing	Xが～するのを禁止する	U12-P6
project	名 事業計画、プロジェクト	U4-P6
promote	動 ～を昇進させる	U8-P7
promptly	副 即座に	U1-P6
pronounce	動 発音する	U3-P7
properly	副 適切に	U11-P2
property	名 不動産、財産	U11-P2
proposal	名 提案、企画	U6-P7
provide	動 ～を提供する	U2-P3
public relations	広報活動、PR	U11-P6
public transportation	名 公共交通機関	U3-P5
publisher	名 出版社、発行者	U10-P7
punctual	形 時間に正確な	U3-P5
purpose	名 目的	U4-P4
put on ～	～を身につける	U5-P3

Q

qualifications	名 資格、適性	U4-P3
quarterly	形 年4回の、3カ月おきの	U4-P7
questionnaire	名 アンケート	U7-P2

R

reach	動 ～に連絡をとる	U6-P4
reception	名 宴会、歓迎会	U2-P2
receptionist	名 受付係	U2-P2
recipe	名 調理法	U5-P5
recognize	動 ～を評価する、認める	U3-P6
recruit	動 ～を採用する	U4-P7
reduce	動 ～を減らす	U11-P7
reference	名 推薦状	U4-P4
refund	名 返金	U3-P4
regarding	前 ～に関しての	U4-P7
register	動 登録する	U9-P7
registration	形 登録	U2-P6
reimbursement	名 返済、払い戻し	U11-P4
reliable	形 信頼できる	U12-P7
relocate	動 ～を移転させる	U8-P4
remind X of ～	Xに～を思い出させる	U2-P3
renovation	名 改築、刷新	U8-P4
repair	動 ～を修理する	U8-P3
replace	動 ～を取り替える	U8-P3
requirement	名 必要要件、資格	U2-P7
reschedule	動 ～の予定を変更する、延期する	U6-P3
researcher	名 調査員	U12-P7
reservation	名 予約	U6-P2
reserve	動 ～を予約する	U10-P7
respond	動 返答する、～と答える	U6-P3
respondent	名 回答者	U2-P5

133

- ☐ responsibility 名 責任、職責 ……… U4-P7
- ☐ restore 動 ～を修復する ……… U7-P5
- ☐ résumé 名 履歴書 ……… U4-P3
- ☐ retailer 名 小売店 ……… U1-P5
- ☐ retire 動 退職する、引退する ……… U12-P4
- ☐ review 名 批評記事、評価 ……… U5-P4
- ☐ revise 動 ～を改訂する、改正する ……… U8-P7
- ☐ ride 動 ～に乗って行く ……… U10-P1
- ☐ rise 名 上昇、増加 ……… U9-P4
- ☐ roadwork 名 道路工事 ……… U3-P6
- ☐ route 名 道、経路 ……… U3-P6
- ☐ routine 形 いつもの、所定の ……… U2-P5
- ☐ rude 形 無礼な、ぶしつけな ……… U5-P7

S

- ☐ sales representative 営業担当、販売代理人 ……… U4-P2
- ☐ savings account 普通預金口座 ……… U11-P3
- ☐ scenery 名 景色、景観 ……… U10-P3
- ☐ secretary 名 秘書 ……… U9-P7
- ☐ serve 動 （食事など）を出す ……… U5-P3
- ☐ server 名 給仕する人 ……… U5-P1
- ☐ set up ～を建てる、準備する ……… U6-P1
- ☐ shipment 名 出荷、発送 ……… U1-P5
- ☐ shop 動 買い物をする ……… U1-P4
- ☐ shopper 名 買い物客 ……… U1-P1
- ☐ sightseeing 名 観光 ……… U10-P2
- ☐ sign 名 看板、標識 ……… U7-P4
- ☐ situation 名 状況、立場 ……… U5-P6
- ☐ solution 名 解決（策） ……… U6-P6
- ☐ spacious 形 広々とした ……… U9-P2
- ☐ spare 形 手の空いた、暇な ……… U2-P7
- ☐ specialize in ～ ～を専門にする ……… U1-P5
- ☐ stack 動 ～を積み重ねる ……… U5-P1
- ☐ stock 名 株式、株（券） ……… U11-P3
- ☐ stock market 株取引、株式市場 ……… U11-P2
- ☐ stop 名 停留所 ……… U3-P2
- ☐ strategy 名 戦略 ……… U9-P3
- ☐ submit 動 ～を提出する ……… U4-P3
- ☐ subscribe to ～ ～を定期購読する ……… U7-P5
- ☐ subway 名 地下鉄 ……… U3-P3
- ☐ suggest 動 ～をそれとなく言う ……… U1-P7
- ☐ suggestion 名 提案 ……… U7-P3
- ☐ suitable 形 適切な、ふさわしい ……… U7-P7
- ☐ supervise 動 ～を監督する、管理する ……… U5-P5
- ☐ supervisor 名 管理者、監督者 ……… U6-P3
- ☐ supplier 名 供給者、納入業者 ……… U4-P7
- ☐ supplies 名 供給品、必需品 ……… U6-P3
- ☐ survey 名 調査 ……… U12-P2
- ☐ suspension 名 （一時的な）停止 ……… U3-P6
- ☐ sweep 動 （ほうきなどで）～を掃く ……… U12-P1

T

- ☐ take care of ～の世話をする ……… U2-P7
- ☐ take charge of ～の責任を負う ……… U4-P7
- ☐ take notes ノートをとる ……… U4-P1
- ☐ take off ～を脱ぐ、はずす ……… U8-P1
- ☐ take over （仕事などを）引き継ぐ ……… U12-P4
- ☐ take part in ～に参加する ……… U9-P4
- ☐ take place 行われる、開催される ……… U9-P3
- ☐ target 名 目標 ……… U4-P7
- ☐ tax 名 税金 ……… U1-P7
- ☐ temperature 名 温度、気温 ……… U2-P4
- ☐ temporary 形 一時的な、臨時の ……… U10-P4
- ☐ temporary staff 派遣社員、臨時社員 ……… U9-P7
- ☐ text 動 （携帯電話で）～にメールを書いて送る ……… U12-P2
- ☐ theater 名 劇場、映画館 ……… U7-P5
- ☐ thought 名 考え ……… U5-P6
- ☐ tip 名 助言、秘訣 ……… U11-P6
- ☐ tourist 名 旅行者 ……… U10-P2
- ☐ traffic 名 交通（量） ……… U2-P4
- ☐ transfer 動 転任する、転勤する ……… U4-P3
- ☐ treat 動 ～を治療する ……… U2-P3
- ☐ turn off （電気など）を消す ……… U2-P1
- ☐ typical 形 典型的な ……… U10-P7

U

- ☐ uniform 名 制服 ……… U8-P2
- ☐ upcoming 形 次の、やって来る ……… U7-P5
- ☐ update 名 最新情報 ……… U8-P6
- ☐ utensils 名 （主に台所の）用具 ……… U8-P6
- ☐ utilities 名 公共料金、公共設備 ……… U11-P7

V

- ☐ vacancy 名 （職などの）欠員 ……… U12-P7
- ☐ vehicle 名 車両、乗り物 ……… U2-P6
- ☐ venue 名 開催地、会場 ……… U9-P5
- ☐ verify 動 （調査などで）～を確かめる ……… U10-P6
- ☐ video conference テレビ会議 ……… U3-P7
- ☐ view 名 眺め、見晴らし ……… U10-P3
- ☐ voicemail 名 留守番電話、音声メール ……… U6-P4

W

- ☐ warehouse 名 倉庫 ……… U1-P4
- ☐ warranty 名 保証 ……… U8-P3
- ☐ water 動 ～に水をやる ……… U7-P1
- ☐ withdraw 動 （お金）を引き出す ……… U11-P2
- ☐ workforce 名 全従業員、労働力 ……… U9-P7
- ☐ workplace 名 職場 ……… U3-P6
- ☐ workshop 名 研修会 ……… U9-P7

Y

- ☐ yet 接 けれども ……… U11-P6

教師用音声CD有り（非売品）

FIRST TIME TRAINER FOR THE TOEIC® TEST
〈Revised Edition〉
はじめてのTOEIC®受験徹底対策
〈改訂版〉

2016年12月20日	初版発行
2025年 1 月30日	第10刷発行

著者	妻鳥 千鶴子／田平 真澄／松井 こずえ
発行	センゲージ ラーニング株式会社
	〒102-0073
	東京都千代田区九段北1-11-11 第2フナトビル5階
	電話　　03-3511-4392
	FAX　　03-3511-4391
	E-mail　eltjapan@cengage.com
制作	株式会社 アスク出版
表紙デザイン	株式会社 アスク デザイン部
本文デザイン・組版	朝日メディアインターナショナル株式会社
イラスト	伊藤 和人
印刷・製本	株式会社 光邦

ISBN 978-4-86312-293-2

もし落丁、乱丁、そのほか不良品がありましたら、お取り替えいたします。
本書の全部または一部を無断で複写（コピー）することは、著作権法上での例外を除き、禁じられていますのでご注意ください。